Demystifying Baldrige

Donald C. Fisher, Ph.D. • **Julie E. Horine, Ph.D.**
Tricia H. Carlisle • **Stephen D. Williford**

Foreword by Frederick W. Smith,
Founder and Chairman of Federal Express Corporation

The Lincoln-Bradley Publishing Group

New York

Memphis   Gatlinburg

Permissions Department
The Lincoln-Bradley Publishing Group
P.O. Box 808
Gatlinburg, TN 37738

Publisher's Cataloging in Publication
(Quality Books, Inc.)

Demystifying Baldrige/Donald C. Fisher... (et.al.);
foreword by Fred Smith.
p. cm.
Includes bibliographical references and index.
ISBN 1-879111-50-0

1. Total quality management – United States – Case
studies. 2. Total quality management – United States –
Handbooks, manuals, etc. 3. Malcolm Baldrige National
Quality Award. I. Fisher, Donald C.

HD62.15.D46 1993   658.5'62

QBI93-615

Printed on approved acid-free paper
Cover Design by Eric Robinette
Book Design and Make-up by Electronic Publishing Services, Inc.
1 2 3 4 5 6 7 8 9 10

Dedication

We dedicate this book to Frederick W. Smith, founder and Chairman of Federal Express Corporation, who continues to champion the quality movement and demystifies the meaning of World Class Leader. When we asked for his help, he said, "Absolutely." The rest is history.

Demystifying Baldrige is available at special quantity discounts. For details regarding quantity purchases, write or telephone:

Special Markets
The Lincoln-Bradley Publishing Group
P.O. Box 808
Gatlinburg, TN 37738
(615) 436-4762

For additional inquiries, you may contact our above business office, or, according to your interests, you may contact us at:

Production Office
The Lincoln-Bradley Publishing Group
305 Madison Avenue – Suite 1166
New York, NY 10165
(212) 953-1125

Editorial Office
The Lincoln-Bradley Publishing Group
3780 S. Mendenhall Road – Suite 206
Memphis, Tennessee 38115
(901) 363-3518

Other Books by The Lincoln-Bradley Publishing Group
Include:

A STRATEGY FOR WINNING
(ISBN 1-879111-75-6)
by *Carl Mays*, with a Foreword by Lou Holtz

THE LONGABERGER STORY – AND HOW WE DID IT
(ISBN 1-879111-25-X)
by *Dave Longaberger*, with Steve Williford

LOSE TO WIN
A CARDIOLOGIST'S GUIDE TO WEIGHT LOSS & NUTRITIONAL HEALING
(ISBN 1-879111-26-8)
by *Stephen T. Sinatra, M.D.*

THE SIMPLIFIED BALDRIGE AWARD ORGANIZATION ASSESSMENT
(ISBN 1-879111-51-9)
by *Donald C. Fisher, Ph.D.*

Table of Contents

Foreword

I believe the challenge for today's leaders is the ability to communicate one's vision in such a way that others understand it and are empowered to pursue it.

We begin to share the vision by creating a workplace that responds to the human desire to be a part of the greater mission – one in which everyone can contribute and make a difference.

I can think of a no more effective corporate strategic plan than one structured around the tenets of the Malcolm Baldrige self assessment. The strategy is to integrate quality throughout the company. This self assessment process must be accurate and thorough, then deployed and measured throughout the company.

Frederick W. Smith
Chairman and Chief Executive Officer
Federal Express

Acknowledgements

As we were writing our book, Bob Waterman was creating a video documentary of the Wallace Company with Enterprise Media, Inc. entitled "Quality Through People." We are grateful for their cooperation in allowing us to excerpt parts of that documentary.

We wish to thank the following organizations and individuals for willingly giving of their time to share their experiences and quality practices with us. First, the leaders of the 1990 Malcolm Baldrige Award winning organizations: Fred Smith of Federal Express Corporation, Larry Osterwise of IBM Rochester, John Wallace of the Wallace Company, and John Grettenberger of Cadillac.

We would like to thank Diane Ritter of GOAL/QPC for her helpful ideas that contributed to our assessment activity, and for sharing the idea of using the radar chart with the Baldrige assessment.

We are also grateful for the generous assistance from Anne Manning at Federal Express; John Akers and Terry Lautenbauch, formerly of IBM; Steve Schwartz and Roy Bauer, formerly of IBM Rochester; Rosetta Riley, Lou Farinola and Pat Adams of Cadillac; Sonny Wallace and Donna Lee, formerly of the Wallace Company; and Michael Spiess, a quality consultant, formerly with the Wallace Company.

Also, thank-you , Sharon Theobold for sitting through many meetings and working through countless manuscript changes.

Preface

It has long been assumed that things that are "simple" aren't as powerful or meaningful as things that are difficult.

We disagree.

Our goal is to simplify the Malcolm Baldrige approach to quality improvement. Removing the veil of confusion and demystifying the application is no easy task.

In an increasingly demanding search for quality, many companies are investing enormous resources and receiving little in return.

Whether your organization is large, small, public, private, domestic or international, this book can help you. This book can be used as a guide or tool for you to translate your vision of excellence into improved customer satisfaction, increased productivity and attainment of bottom line goals.

We begin our demystification process by examining America's battered business track record and quality's role in our come-back. We think you'll find some interesting corporate examples and some surprising statistics.

After setting the stage for quality, we then look at the role of the Malcolm Baldrige Self Assessment. In the chapter, *The Baldrige Dilemma*, we examine the "Top 11 Reasons" for not using the Baldrige. In the following chapter, *The Baldrige Solution*, we look at the self assessment's advantages and address each of the 11 objections. By the way, we even agree with one of them!

The next four chapters represent four separate case studies of how companies used the Baldrige Self Assessment and applied quality principles. As a part of our Baldrige Demystification research, we selected certain Baldrige winning companies to further investigate. We found it very interesting that all four of the 1990 award winning companies experienced problems either with their own organization, such as the Wallace Company and Federal Express, or within their parent company, such as Cadillac's parent General Motors Corporation and IBM Rochester's parent IBM Corporation.

So, we decided to investigate each of these companies, to interview their senior executives and to demystify first hand the way of the winners. The diversity and scope of each of these businesses further exemplify the applicable nature of the Malcolm Baldrige criteria.

Although the previous material is prerequisite before going further, the most practical and exciting part of the book begins with the chapter *A User Friendly Self Assessment*. We show, step by step, how we suggest to conduct a self assessment. *The Best of the Best* includes our "Key Characteristics for World Class Leadership," and a Self Assessment and Action Plan for leaders within your organization. *A Bottom Line Prediction* looks at your return on investment for performing a Baldrige Self Assessment. Finally, we provide a wealth of reference information which we trust will keep this book close to your desk at least during your self assessment process.

No one can really predict the future for American business. We can examine economic indicators and contract records and take a hard look at the CEO, but there's no guarantee of the success rate. But one thing's for sure. The "future" will never be like the past.

The future *promises* to bring about change. Changes that require new priorities, new and creative thinking, new ways to respond. It's what the Japanese have been doing for the past 40 years. It's what businesses of the future must do to stay competitive, and that thinking is a focus on quality. Without *quality* the corporate race for survival will be lost.

We recognize that "running the race" on the fast track requires preparation, training and a gut-wrenching self assessment. As you run your own race for *quality*, this text is designed to inform you, help you think in a new way and give you the tools for a company self assessment. In some ways, it's a map to guide you on the road to achieving quality. Whether you decide to embrace the Malcolm Baldrige criteria as a prize or a template, you will be a winner. Self examination yields valuable dividends and guarantees a place in the winner's lane.

We wish you success as you look into your own quality future and begin the race.

Winning the Malcolm Baldrige National Quality Award was rewarding, but only consistent quality standards will maintain customer loyalty. Quality is not complicated. But it must be totally integrated and extremely consistent.

Rosetta Riley
Member of the 1993 Panel of Judges,
The Malcolm Baldrige National Quality Award
Director of Customer Satisfaction
North American Operations
General Motors Corporation

Chapter ONE

POISED ON THE EDGE

It's more than a "buzz word." *Quality* has become the survival issue of the 90's. American companies now recognize that poor quality costs as much as 20 percent of revenues. Businesses are beginning to equate quality goods and services with improved productivity, lower costs and increased profitability.

Over the past two decades, the United States' leadership in product and process quality has been inundated by relentless foreign competition. Countries such as Japan and Germany have improved the quality of their goods and services, while the quality of many American goods and services declined. During this same time period, America's historically competitive edge in productivity has eroded.

Changing customer requirements now demands shorter cycle times in bringing new innovations to the marketplace. Even the traditional ways of managing organizations are being challenged and replaced with "total quality management." Businesses are beginning to recognize that to remain competitive in tomorrow's global marketplace, they must now focus on quality in both products and services.

THE BALDRIGE AWARD – A CATALYST FOR QUALITY FOCUS

In a national effort to stimulate quality and productivity, and to recognize U.S. companies for their quality achievements, the Malcolm Baldrige National Quality Award was enacted into law (Public Law 100-107) by Congress in 1987.

The award is named for the late Secretary of Commerce and calls for the creation of a national quality award and the development of guidelines and criteria that organizations could use to assess their quality improvement efforts. Up to two awards may be given each year in three major categories: Manufacturing, Service and Small Business.

During its first years, the Baldrige Award program has focused national and international attention on the quality of goods and services. Canada, Mexico, Brazil and Sweden have patterned their own national quality award programs after the Baldrige Award.

At least 30 states have created their own quality awards modeled after the Baldrige, sometimes called "Baby Baldriges." Many of the state awards have expanded the Baldrige categories to include categories for health care, education and government. Kenmore-Town of Tonawanda School District in upstate New York became the first school system nationally to receive a "Baby Baldrige" quality award when it was awarded New York's *Excelsior Award* in 1992.

The Baldrige Award requires the winners to share successful quality strategies with other companies. The sharing partnership promotes a "win-win" philosophy previously unprecedented in American business.

"In just a few years," noted former President Bush, "the National Quality Award has literally become the standard of business excellence... it has become a road map for U.S. companies on their journey of continuously improving quality."

The National Institute of Standards and Technology (NIST), along with industry experts, developed the seven category, 1000 point scoring system and the three level judging process. Companies submit applications from 50 to 75 pages, depending on company size, detailing and documenting their quality practices and performance in each of the seven areas. Applications are then evaluated independently by trained examiners.

The Baldrige examiners, who donate their time, are recruited from the private and public sectors. The Board of Judges selects high scoring applicants for site visits. A team of examiners visits each company for several days. They conduct extensive interviews and check documentation. The judges then meet to review top applicants and select the winners. The entire process takes over six months, not counting the time to prepare the application.

To win the award a company must have a World Class system for managing its processes and its people. This system's goal is to ensure continuous improvement of products or services and provide a way of satisfying customer requirements. The end result is improved quality of products and services and increased customer satisfaction.

The Baldrige National Award is recognized as the most prestigious and coveted prize in American business. It represents the most intensive and objective corporate assessment.

AND THE WINNERS ARE...

A total of 17 companies (company divisions or plant sites) have won the award since 1987:

1992 Award Winners

- AT&T Network Systems Group/ Transmissions Systems Business Unit
- Texas Instruments, Inc./ Defense Systems & Electronics Group
- AT&T Universal Card Services
- Ritz-Carlton Hotel Company
- Granite Rock Company

1991 Award Winners

- Solectron Corporation
- Zytec Corporation
- Marlow Industries

1990 Award Winners

- Cadillac Motor Car Company
- IBM Rochester
- Federal Express Corporation
- Wallace Company

1989 Award Winners

- Milliken & Company
- Xerox Business Products and Systems

1988 Award Winners

- Motorola, Inc.
- Westinghouse Commercial – Nuclear Fuel Division
- Globe Metallurgical, Inc.

We feel that one of the more beneficial requirements is that winners must share information about their successful quality strategies with other American organizations. However, the amount of time and effort is decided by the companies. Winners are invited to participate in the award's annual excellence conference, provide materials on their quality strategies and to respond to news media's inquiries. That may not seem like a huge task, but over 20,000 telephone calls alone were logged by one recent winner.

Chapter
TWO

A SURVIVAL ISSUE

By the year 2000, corporate America will have thinned out.

It will be the survival of the fittest. As we have seen, there will be fewer conglomerates, more small businesses and a proliferation of cottage industries. This forced evolution is the consequence of the way we have been doing business for the past 50 years. Like the dinosaurs in the Le Brea Tar Pits, we will be unable to avoid extinction if we do not change the way we do business.

This evolutionary process has been costly. From an industrialization of the 50's and 60's to the high-tech 90's, change has occurred rapidly and fiercely. Those companies that couldn't compete were left along the side of the road.

At times it appeared business was out of control. Institutions that we depended on were left out in the cold. The 80's and 90's are witness to the dissolution of the banking industry, the collapse of major airlines and corporate giants being taken over by leveraged buy-outs.

So what does that have to do with the Malcolm Baldrige National Quality Award?

The Malcolm Baldrige Award was created as a direct result of America's crash from world leadership. It was a formal recognition that change had to occur. If not, casualties would be high and some of the greatest companies and CEO's would be fatalities.

In October 21, 1990 issue of *The Detroit Free Press*, editorialist Paul Lienert commiserated:

> My family and my neighbors have been affected directly by the decade-long decline of the American auto industry. On a more personal level, every consumer purchase decision, from watches and cameras to automobiles, must be weighed and not just in terms of its impact on the economy. For instance, do I buy the Japanese car for my family and expect it to run flawlessly from the

start - and feel guilty for helping put fellow Americans out of work - or do I buy the homegrown product, knowing from experience that it may not have the same quality and may require more frequent repairs and service? Call me a closet patriot, but I feel much better about buying American products when the U.S. manufacturers give me a reason to feel good.

It's true enough that in recent years corporate executives have paid constant lip service to such notions as customer satisfaction and vehicle quality. Too often, however, independent studies and personal experiences don't bear out the public pronouncements. Getting the new quality message across to the public is critical. Too many people have been burned too often by domestic manufacturers and their dealers.

Hundreds of thousands of once loyal car buyers who felt alienated by the 'big three' have turned to imports for security and peace of mind. It's going to be an uphill battle, especially with the prevailing 'boy who cried wolf' image that still saddles the U.S. firms. Yet, I'm convinced that most Americans would rather buy American products if they believe that they don't have to sacrifice quality or value.

Honors such as the Baldrige Award will help reinforce a more positive image for the domestic industry. It's enough to lure a would-be patriot out the closet to do a little flag waving.

Perhaps the biggest surprise is the fact that **customers** are not loyal to a **company** or even to a **country**. They're loyal to **quality**.

In 1960, the United States' share of World GNP was 35%. Japan's was 3%. In 1980, our GNP share was down a third to 22% while Japan's was up by **over 300%** to 10%.

Akio Morita, Co-founder of Sony Corporation, made this observation: "American companies either shifted output to low-wage countries or came to buy parts and assembled products from countries like Japan that could make **quality** products at low prices. The result was a **hollowing** of American industry. The U.S. was abandoning its status as an industrial power. We weren't taking away your manufacturers' business. **You gave it up.**"

How did we give it up? According to a June 1987 *Business Week* Special Report, the typical American factory invested an unbelievable 20 to 25% of its operating budget in **simply finding and fixing mistakes!** That is to say that as many as **one fourth** of *all* factory workers didn't **make anything at all**... They just redid what wasn't done right the first time.

Add to that the expense of repairing or replacing the flawed products, and the cost of ignoring quality was close to a third of production costs. While the Japanese were creating a stable economy, we were burying ourselves economically.

The number one problem of U.S. competitiveness was **poor quality**.

The story goes that a production worker was asked, "What's the difference between ignorance and apathy?"

The man replied, **"I don't know and I don't care."**

That attitude permeated from the top down. Few gave quality much thought.

The diagnosis was grim. The prescription had to be dramatic.

Companies had to prioritize quality. To do so required a total re-engineering. It often involved drastic change in corporate culture, management philosophy and employee attitude.

And it wasn't just the assembly line worker who had to face change; change had to begin at the very top.

If United States businesses didn't improve their quality, we would lose by default. There would be no markets in which to compete.

Steve Schwartz, retired Senior Vice President of Market Driven Quality at IBM, notes, "Quality is a subject that's on everyone's mind. It's a survival issue. During the 1990's, quality will make the difference between success and failure... and it will require the transformation of the way we do business."

Until the mid-1980's, like many companies, corporate giant IBM focused on the product instead of the customer, on creating the product and then working to create demand for the product. It measured success by product volumes, revenue and profit margin. But it was rapidly losing industry market share. A quick fix was needed but none worked.

Although the reports appeared dark, there **was** light on the horizon. Some industries slowly recognized the missing equation and committed to the prescription of quality.

QUALITY IS CREATED

Whether we liked it or not, we learned a strong lesson from Japan. Quality does not just happen. It is created.

U.S. companies began a quest for a higher level of quality from their employees and suppliers. For example, Xerox found itself rapidly losing market share to the Japanese in 1983. The reason was simple: Japanese copiers cost less and were more reliable. Ninety-two percent of the parts from Xerox suppliers were defect-free, which left Xerox apologizing to customers for not getting good copies almost 10% of the time.

Xerox Chairman David Kearns recognized the need to re-engineer the way Xerox was doing business. He declared quality improvement to be the company's driving principle. Xerox trained all of its employees in quality. Xerox reduced its number of suppliers by developing a supplier certification program. Those suppliers who could not meet the stringent certification requirements were removed. Their efforts were rewarded. In 1989, Xerox was awarded the Malcolm Baldrige.

Today, over **99.7%** of Xerox parts are defect-free. Their ultimate goal is **no** defects per million.

That's not as far-fetched as it might sound. Several Xerox suppliers have shipped **no defective part for years**. Overall, it meant dramatic sales increases to Xerox, reduced costs and increased reliability to the customer.

Fred Martin, President of Dobbs International, a national airline caterer, maintains that 99% quality is not good enough. He likes to tell this story to emphasize how strongly he feels about consumer-based quality.

"Two colleagues and I were on final approach into Memphis. I could hear the nose gear wheel keep going down, then up, and we aborted our landing. The pilot informed us that according to the control panel light, the wheel wasn't locked.

"He said, 'We're going for a fly-by to get visual verification from our people in the tower.' We did and he came back on to inform us that it wasn't locked into position. 'But,' he said, 'we have our best engineers and mechanics reviewing the situation and we should have an answer soon.' In the meantime, we were asked to remove our shoes and jewelry.

"The co-pilot came back in the cabin, ripped up the carpet, opened a door in the floor, stuck his head in and said, 'It **looks** locked.'

"Then the pilot said, 'Ladies and gentlemen, we've talked to our ground personnel and we're **99% certain** that the wheel is locked. But just to be on the safe side, we'd like for everyone to assume the crash position.'

"Well, we landed with no difficulty and watched the fire and emergency personnel chase us down the runway. As we were taxiing to our gate we commented to each other that **a 99% guarantee isn't satisfactory to a customer in mid-air!**"

So What Is Quality?

"*Succeeding* into the 1990's and beyond" was an often heard catch phrase of business during the first year of the new decade. But many futurists say, "*Quality* is the true war cry of the 90's." Without quality, there is no success. It's energizing. It rallies the troops and gives form to function. But for many companies, it's a desperation move, like open heart surgery; the arteries need to be unclogged so new life blood can flow into the body. The life blood is quality.

John Wallace, former CEO of the Wallace Company, 1990 Malcolm Baldrige National Quality Award Winner, says that "quality is an all-encompassing way of doing business which leads to customer satisfaction. Quality demands 100% commitment to the process from 100% of the organization and it starts at the top."

Quality keeps the customer and empowers the employee.

Quality is the fifth missing element in the world. Earth, wind, water, fire and quality. The basics which we take for granted. Without quality, there is no customer, therefore there is no business.

Quality is the bottom line, the naked truth, the bare bones. It's doing an in-depth soul search of your company.

Quality is not something you can go out and buy. Nor is it some kind of magic chant, where you can say, "Voilla! So be it!" and wave a magic wand. It is the ability to create standards and measurements for any organization. Quality is accepting responsibility for those findings and defining solutions. Quality is created; it's nurtured through strong leadership and integrated throughout an organization.

Quality is the only capable rationale that will stabilize American companies and organizations in the next decade.

Quality is Unjustly Defined

At a recent planning meeting of senior executives, the subject was "Raise the Bar" (an allusion to raising the bar in the high jump in track). The chairperson asked, "What are your expectations? What are your goals?" The entire meeting was on goals, but no mention was made of how to obtain them. The philosophy was, if you know the goals, you'll find a way to get there.

Noted author Tom Peters defines quality by telling us what it isn't. "Quality is not a technique. It is above all, about **care**... **people**... **passion**... **consistency**... **eyeball contact** and **gut reaction**. Devices to maintain quality are valuable only if managers – at **all** levels – **are living the quality message**.

"Quality comes from the belief that **anything** can be made better. Quality involves **living** the message."

Quality expert Philip Crosby puts it this way: "Quality is free. It's not a gift but it **is** free. What costs money are all the **non-quality** things – all the actions that involve not doing jobs right the first time. Making quality certain means getting people to do better all the worthwhile things they **ought to be doing anyway**. Managers can improve quality. They can prevent programming errors, burred screws, cold steaks, lost parcels and miscalculated bills.

"Quality is not **only** free, it is a **profit maker**. Every penny you **don't** spend on doing things wrong, over or instead, becomes **half a penny on the bottom line**. If you concentrate on **making quality happen**, you can probably increase your profit by an amount equal to five to ten percent of your sales. That's a lot of money for free."

Jaguar was a classic case of poor quality. The factory was over manned, filled with outdated machinery and ineffectively managed. In 1980, they were averaging only 1.3 cars per employee annually and losing **1.5 million dollars** a week. Production had fallen from 32,000 cars in 1974 to less than 14,000 in 1980. Sales in the United States had dropped from over 7,000 in 1976 to 3,000 in 1980.

A rather tacit joke at the time was, "If you're going to buy a Jaguar, you better buy **two** so you'll have something to drive while the **other one's** in the shop."

J.D. Powers and Associates, a market research company, couldn't even **include** Jaguar in their published automaker's satisfaction report because so few customers would **admit** to owning a Jag. The cars not only represented poor quality work, but the company regularly missed model year deadlines not by days... not by weeks... by **months**!

In our opinion, if ever there was a shining example of what poor quality can do, it was Jaguar. John Egan, formerly with Massey-Ferguson manufacturing company, was persuaded to become Jaguar's new Chairman and CEO. His mission was to save Jaguar or close it.

Egan realized that if Jaguar was to be saved, it would have to be done in the U.S. He studied Jaguar's problems for six months and made radical changes in the factory. He established **240** areas in need of improvement and stunned dealers by **pointing out** those problems, ranging from leaking steering gears to peeling paint. The dealers' reaction, by the way, was **positive**. They felt that recognizing and admitting the problems was the first step toward Jaguar's survival.

One of the most frustrating problems had been shortages of spare parts for repairs. Egan threatened to stop the production line rather than send cars to the U.S. without adequate parts backup. As a result, the production managers did whatever was necessary to take care of the problem.

Jaguar began a quality tracking program in which an independent research firm telephoned several hundred buyers a month and tracked their ownership experiences for three years. Some of the conversations were taped and gave this scenario of what it meant to own a Jaguar: dirty service department waiting rooms, incompetent mechanics and indifferent dealers. The tapes were played to middle management and then to service managers, who in turn contacted the customers to resolve complaints.

Top management monitored the process by also asking customers if their problems had been handled satisfactorily. For any that **weren't**, one of the senior vice-presidents would **personally** escort the customer to the dealer and say, "We're going to address this problem on the spot. Give the customer a car and let him (or her) drive away." The message came through loud and clear. **Customer satisfaction was a priority**.

Through Egan's efforts, factories and waiting rooms were **scrubbed and cleaned**, personnel received more training and cars began arriving **regularly and on time**.

Warranty costs fell because less repairs were needed. **Pride and enthusiasm started to surface, too**. For the first time in 20 years, employees started to **boast** about working for Jaguar. And with good reason.

J.D. Powers now includes Jaguar as one of the best ranking cars in car-buyer satisfaction.

Quality is a survival issue. Customers are loyal not to a product or company, but to quality.

Chapter THREE

THE BALDRIGE DILEMMA

The first step to implementing quality in an organization is to perform a self assessment such as the Baldrige. Yet, not all companies are willing to use this tool. So before we go further, let's examine some objections to using the Baldrige. Organizations offer many reasons for not using the Baldrige self assessment. We rated these as the top 11.

THE TOP 11 REASONS NOT TO USE THE MALCOLM BALDRIGE SELF ASSESSMENT

#1. Few companies complete the application process. Each year, over 150,000 copies of the application are requested but only around 100 applications are submitted, for a dismal return rate – less than one tenth of one percent!

#2. Bottom-line results from the Malcolm Baldrige self assessment don't occur immediately and may *cost* before they contribute to the bottom line. Some companies aren't willing to make that commitment.

#3. Because it is government-related, some people view the Baldrige Award as short-lived or a reaction to Japanese quality movement.

#4. For many, the application is mind boggling, time consuming and intimidating. The language in each question is hard to understand. Therefore, confusion abounds on how to correctly complete the assessment, creating an unnecessary mystique.

As a matter of fact, a popular applicants' insider joke is:

> *Question: What's the hardest thing about winning the Malcolm Baldrige Award?*
>
> *Answer: Filling out the application.*

The complexity of the process has created a great deal of confusion, corporate mental fog and befuddlement. What should be a *tool*, often becomes a hindrance. It requires bringing in a "defogging consultant."

#5. Winning the award is a symbol of prestige. It doesn't mean anything.

#6. It's a large financial and time commitment.

#7. Some companies see this as a last ditch effort.

#8. Many firms believe they can achieve the same reputation as the winners simply by duplicating steps, activities, programs and systems of winners.

#9. One successful entrepreneur shared this impression of the Baldrige process, "Malcolm Baldrige? Who needs it? You don't need somebody else to tell you how to run your business."

#10. Malcolm Baldrige quality won't last.

#11. Quality will eliminate jobs.

"YOU CAN'T MAKE ME!"

We've found a lot of resistance to the Malcolm Baldrige Self Assessment process. We've heard these additional rationales for not performing a Baldrige assessment (they didn't make the top 11, but they're worthy as runner-ups):

- Our company is very profitable.
- Just because the measurement indicated that morale is bad, how do we know that we didn't *improve* from last year?
- We experience very few customer complaints.
- We already have a 60% share of the market – that's all we can handle.
- Yes, quality is important, but we've got some other things on the front burner right now.
- We already are a quality company. We have a quality day and print quality T-shirts.
- We're not ready yet.
- We couldn't get the management team to agree.
- The employees won't understand the process.
- We're too big/small to do it.
- We're too spread out. There is no one available to do it.
- It might work for others, but not for us.
- We don't like to receive a grade.

YOU DON'T NEED IT IF...

The Baldrige assessment creates an accountability process which will reveal weaknesses. If a manager is not doing a good job, the assessment will probably indicate it. *Therefore, to the incompetent, the lazy or the indifferent, the Malcolm Baldrige can represent trouble – it may well identify who is not contributing to the total quality process.*

If you don't believe that business leaders are struggling in the global marketplace, you don't need it.

If you don't believe that innovative, quality products and services at lower costs require teamwork to meet the changing needs of customers, you don't need it.

If you don't believe the Malcolm Baldrige criteria enable organizations to identify strengths and weaknesses and provide a basis for reshaping thinking and behavior, you don't need it.

You should quit reading here. Just watch TV.

Chapter
FOUR

THE BALDRIGE SOLUTION

With the previous chapter's objectives in mind, the question must be asked, "Why use the Malcolm Baldrige Self Assessment?"

For many visionary leaders, the Baldrige offers a framework to help eliminate problems and create solutions.

Curt W. Reimann, Director of the MBNQA program in Gaithersburg, MD, offers, "the Baldrige is a participative, non-prescriptive program rather than a forced march to quality. The criteria provide a definition of total quality while helping a company generate evidence of progress."

Federal Express' former COO Jim Barksdale reflected, "The Malcolm Baldrige preparation process was extremely rigorous and helped us take a very close look at ourselves and our quality processes. We discovered many things we could be doing better. Continuous quality improvement is the only way to put the United States products and services at the forefront of the global marketplace and to help keep them there!"

Robert Stempel, former General Motors CEO, adds, "This award verifies that our processes are in place and that customer satisfaction is the number one goal."

Cadillac's Plant Manager, John Grettenberger, surmises, "Winning the award is a measuring point from which we have to improve."

John Wallace, Wallace Company's former CEO, says, "The award helped to rally employees around a common objective."

But they are all in agreement, the real winner of the Baldrige is the American consumer.

DEMYSTIFYING THE TOP 11 REASONS FOR NOT USING THE BALDRIGE

Demystifying the myths is never an easy venue, especially when there is a hint of truth in each of them. The rebuttal to the detractors of the Malcolm Baldrige is simple – quality begets quality, no matter what the motive.

#1. *Less than one tenth of one percent of requested applications are returned.* Yes, many Baldrige applications are requested. Because they're not returned does not mean they aren't used. Many companies, when embarking on the road to quality, use the application as an initial self assessment tool.

Over 700,000 copies of the criteria have been distributed, not counting the hundreds of thousands of copies made by others, since the Award Program began in 1988. The Baldrige award-winning companies have shared information on their successful quality strategies with hundreds of thousands of companies, educational institutions, government agencies, health care organizations and others. By sharing their quality strategies, award winners have made enormous contributions to building awareness of the importance of quality to our nation's competitiveness.

#2. *Bottom-line results don't occur immediately and may cost before they contribute.* This depends upon what the bottom line would be without the Baldrige. Cost is irrelevant if it's saving you money.

#3. *It's government related.* Just because something is government-originated does not mean it's trendy or short-lived. If it is "only" a reaction to the way the Japanese do business, we are fortunate to have awakened to their way of doing business.

#4. *The application is mind boggling, time consuming and intimi-dating.* A truism. You can't win 'em all!

#5. *Winning the award is a symbol of prestige.* Regardless of the motive, any company that improves is already a winner.

#6. *It's a large financial and time commitment.* Large budgets are not required. Hard work is.

#7. *Some companies see this as a last ditch effort.* So what? Last ditch effort is still effort. Ask the Wallace Company.

#8. *Many firms believe they can achieve the same reputation as the winners simply by duplicating steps, activities, programs and systems of winners.* Benchmarking is the highest form of copying, but you have to be cognizant of your method and purpose. Blind faith is never the answer.

#9. *Who needs it? You don't need somebody else to tell you how to run your business.* Tell that to the out of work bankers, real estate developers and car manufacturers. Also, many companies are now requiring their suppliers to prove their quality credentials by completing the Baldrige self assessment, or companies are conducting an assessment of their suppliers using the MBNQA.

#10. *Malcolm Baldrige quality won't last.* If the MBNQA only does one thing – to raise quality awareness – then it succeeds. Companies that benefit from integrating quality establish infrastructure. They do not go back to slipshod, non-measurable standards.

#11. *Quality will eliminate jobs.* The Malcolm Baldrige quality self assessment empowers employees and drives fear out of the workplace. It's the deployment of quality values that creates job security because an employee knows that he's doing a very important job right the first time.

No, the Malcolm Baldrige is not easy. It's not a quick fix. But it provides an effective framework from which a company may assess itself in seven critical areas. The categories help define in what ways a company can improve.

OUR RESEARCH OF SELECTED MALCOLM BALDRIGE WINNING COMPANIES

As a part of our Baldrige Demystification research, we selected certain Baldrige winning companies to further investigate. We found it very interesting that all four of the 1990 award winning companies experienced problems either within their own organization, such as the Wallace Company and Federal Express, or within their parent company, such as Cadillac's parent General Motors Corporation and IBM Rochester's parent IBM Corporation.

So, we decided to visit each of these companies personally, interview their senior executives, and to demystify first hand the way of the winners. The diversity and scope of each of these businesses further exemplify the applicable nature of the Malcolm Baldrige criteria.

For example, *Cadillac* is the first automaker to receive the Baldrige. *IBM Rochester* site develops and manufactures the AS/400 family of mini-computers. *Federal Express*, the first service company winner, delivers high priority packages. *Wallace* is an industrial distribution company. Both Cadillac and IBM Rochester are divisions of two of the world's largest corporations – General Motors and International Business Machines.

As much as the companies differ, the concepts that guide their approaches to quality improvement are remarkably similar. These winners share five main tenets:

- leadership drives their total quality efforts.
- quality is part of every work process.
- improvement must be customer driven.
- employee buy-in is essential.
- successful improvement strategies must have a long term focus.

Using similar approaches, the goals for each company were different:

Cadillac recognized the need to increase the customer focus. It wanted – no, needed – customer satisfaction, because it didn't have it! It recognized dealers as customers and included them in the quality process. *We think Cadillac's new challenge by the year 2,000 is to attract a new base of younger customers.*

IBM Rochester needed to increase its market share. It was searching for a way to create market driven quality. It had to define the market's needs, create a system for consistently eliminating defects and cycle time, while increasing employee participation. *We see IBM's new challenge for the year 2,000 is to duplicate Rochester's quality-participatory environment throughout the entire organization.*

The Wallace Company entered quality at the "request" (ultimatum) of a customer. Given the fact that Wallace was on the edge of economic disaster, the company was willing to try anything. But once Wallace accepted the quality challenge, it had to totally restructure its business philosophy and operating procedures. For example, assumptions had to be replaced with factual data. This infrastructure allowed them not only to isolate and identify problems, but it also helped Wallace to dramatically increase product consistency. *We see its challenge for the year 2,000 is identifying new niches in its recent merger with B.F. Shaw.*

Federal Express has always been innovative in the company's measurement standards. Already immersed in the quality movement, embracing the Baldrige was a natural progression, and one that helped Federal Express identify, correct and eliminate problems. *We predict its challenge for the year 2,000 is to continue to innovate to maintain the company's edge in an increasingly competitive global marketplace.*

Chapter
FIVE

FEDERAL EXPRESS GEARS UP

It's hard to go anywhere without seeing a purple and orange Federal Express truck, van or plane. When you hear the words, "absolutely, positively," what comes to mind? Probably the many Federal Express commercials that included, "When it absolutely, positively has to be there overnight, call Federal Express."

Federal Express Corporation was the first service company to win the Malcolm Baldrige Quality Award. However, quality was not born overnight at Federal Express. As Frederick W. Smith, Chairman and Chief Executive Officer, phrases it, "Quality is not new nor has it been overnight. We've focused on 100% error free service delivery since Day One. Quality service is really what we are selling.

"More and more we make our own buying decisions based on quality. I think we can all agree, no matter what business we're in, the goal is quality and the challenge is reaching it."

In 1973, Federal Express launched the air-express industry with a fleet of eight small aircraft. Five years later, the company employed 10,000 people, who handled a daily volume of 35,000 shipments. Today, approximately 90,000 Federal Express employees, at more than 1,650 sites, process approximately 1.7 million shipments daily, all of which must be tracked in a central information system, sorted in a short time at facilities in Memphis, Indianapolis, Newark, Oakland, Los Angeles and Anchorage and delivered by a highly decentralized distribution network. The firm's air cargo fleet is now the world's largest.

As former Senior Vice-President Frank Maguire recalls, "That first night, eight planes landed. Sixteen packages. That's right, sixteen. Eight of them were sent by us. We lost one million dollars a month for 27 months before we made a profit. The pilots had to use their own credit cards to pay for gas. Industry experts and potential investors laughed us off. 'Let me get this straight. You're going to take packages from Omaha and Buffalo and Orlando and Bangor and Seattle and San Diego and bring them all into *where? Memphis?* Right. Well, assuming anyone in those cities will trust their packages to you, there's no way you can put a national system together – and Memphis is a stupid idea, too.'"

By adhering constantly to a management philosophy emphasizing *People, Service and Profit*, the company achieved high levels of customer satisfaction. Annual revenues exceeded a phenomenal one billion dollars within 10 years of the company's founding and totaled seven billion dollars in fiscal year 1990. Through a quality improvement focus on 12 Service Quality Indicators (SQI), all tied to the customer, and deployed to all levels of its business, the Memphis-based firm continues to set higher standards for service and customer satisfaction.

CORE VALUES

Federal Express was founded on the core value of customer-driven quality. Before Federal Express even opened its doors, two independent market research studies were conducted by Fred Smith in the mid-1960's to determine the requirements of customers in an air-express delivery service. This chapter highlights the core values embodied by Federal Express, particularly its values of employee participation, customer-driven quality and continuous improvement.

Federal Express exhibits World Class Leadership from its CEO to the entire Senior Executive team. Employees are empowered to solve customer complaints in a short amount of time. People, service and profit is a corporate religion that's exhibited throughout the organization.

A VISION PREVAILS

Federal Express did not begin with a smooth take-off.

The entire venture began with the vision of Smith who wrote a paper while a student at Yale, outlining his early organizational plans for an overnight air delivery service. As the popular story goes, the paper received a 'C.' Smith laughs, "I really don't remember my final grade. Years ago, a reporter asked when I conceived this idea of an overnight delivery service. I related that it began with a paper I wrote for a professor at Yale. He asked me what grade I received for the paper. I stated that I probably received a 'B' or 'C.' Thus began our corporate folklore of my receiving a 'C' on my idea. I've never disposed of the story even though I really don't remember my final grade."

The early days at Federal Express were turmoil-ridden. We heard and read numerous stories of how dedicated Federal Express employees went above and beyond the call of duty to keep Federal Express afloat. For example, we heard about an employee who pawned jewelry to buy fuel for delivery vans; we heard about pilots who used personal credit cards to buy fuel for their aircraft, and even how Fred Smith flew to Las Vegas and gambled to meet the weekly payroll. Smith relates, "The stories sound good, but some of them *did* get a little exaggerated."

PEOPLE – SERVICE – PROFIT PHILOSOPHY

All members of management are held accountable for a *people-first* attitude, excellence in *service* to external and internal customers and to a *profit*, which can be used to recognize employees and improve the company.

As Smith says, "Our corporate philosophy statement – People – Service – Profit – is the key to our success. Three simple words... easy to say... easy to remember... *hard to DO.*

"Obviously, 'people first' is not unique to Federal Express. In fact, I've never heard of a company that says it's *not* a People company. Have you? The problem is that consistently keeping people first is hard work," Smith explained. His eyes sparkled when he talked about the people of Federal Express. You could feel the enthusiasm in his voice. "People come in two very important forms in any company: first and foremost are our customers, and first and foremost are our employees. I'm not sure there's a second place when it comes to people."

Such a battle cry of *people* first in every action, every planning process, every business decision, requires an extraordinary commitment from every Federal Express employee or the philosophy fails. Senior Leadership at Federal Express believes that customer satisfaction begins with employee satisfaction.

The next word in the corporate philosophy is *service*. We heard over and over what the Federal Express *Manager's Guide* says: "If we take care of our employees, they'll take care of our customers. They'll do whatever it takes to get the job done. The strategy is clear: Motivated employees provide better customer service."

Smith puts it this way, "The message our Senior Leadership wants to communicate to our people is: 'We want to obtain and *keep* customers.'"

This provides the last part of Federal Express' philosophy – *profit*. The Senior Leadership at Federal Express sees profit as the result of delivering above average service by a motivated work force.

HIGH STANDARDS OF SERVICE

Customers have come to depend upon Federal Express' high standards of service. They expect shipments to be picked up and delivered on time and arrive in the same condition in which the packages were sent. They expect to be able to pick up the phone at any time during a package's shipment and be told where the package is at that moment. Federal Express believes high levels of service and reliability, coupled with its package tracking system, separates it from the competition.

Smith consistently stresses that customers deserve to be informed. Federal Express receives high marks from its customers because of this ethic.

SERVICE CAN BE MEASURED

Federal Express believes that service can be measured and preaches that service companies can find ways to measure for improvement. The company's methods of measurement include two straightforward quality goals: 100% customer satisfaction for every transaction and 100% service performance on every package.

HOW FEDERAL EXPRESS MEASURES QUALITY

Federal Express' Service Standard is 100% customer satisfaction. Customers expect their packages to arrive on time and undamaged. With over 1.7 million packages being handled daily, even a one percent failure rate could result in 17,000 dissatisfied customers – really 34,000 disgruntled folks when you consider the sender and the receiver. The Service Quality Indicators (SQI) Index helps management review the main areas of their customers' perception of service and how they are meeting them. The Service Quality Indicator was introduced in 1988 and evolved from the old "hierarchy of horrors," or the most common customer complaints. The SQI is a system-wide measure of daily performance which pinpoints the actual number of errors and acts as a guide to reduce this number.

Tom Oliver, Executive Vice President of Customer Operations, was instrumental in developing the SQI process. He explains, "Customers are not only impacted by on-time delivery of their document or package, but they also expect us to answer their questions about package location, provide an accurate bill and receive the package intact. Clearly, the single standard of on-time delivery was inadequate. So, based on historical customer data gained from customers' letters and surveys, we developed a list of 12 items which cause customer dissatisfaction. We had to change our paradigm of what success meant."

Smith says, "The SQI index has helped us to make extraordinary improvements in actual service. There is no question that we measure service with a more reliable, timely process than any of our competitors. The SQI index has also helped us change our thinking, from looking at service quality as a *percentage* of on-time deliveries, to looking at it as the *actual* number of service failures that occurs on a given day. I believe this change in thinking has made a profound difference in our perceptions of how we are performing, and as a result, we have radically improved our delivery of service to the customer."

The Service Quality Indicators are a 12 item quantitative measurement of customer satisfaction and service quality, from the *customer's* perspective.

The indicators and their weights are as follows:

Indicator	Weight
Abandoned Calls	1
Complaints Reopened	5
Damaged Packages	10
International	1
Invoice Adjustments Requested	1
Lost Packages	10
Missed Pick-ups	10
Missing Proofs of Delivery	1
Overgoods (Lost and Found)	5
Right Day Late Deliveries	1
Traces	1
Wrong Day Late Deliveries	5

Every day, Federal Express tracks the individual cumulative SQI score. The Indicators are weighted by the impact on the customer.

Abandoned Calls. Uncompleted. After ten seconds, the caller hangs up.

Complaints Reopened. The initial complaint is not satisfactorily resolved, and thus, reopened.

Damaged Packages. Obvious or concealed damage.

International. Total score of international SQI's.

Invoice Adjustment Requested. Based on the number of package invoice adjustments requested, which represents customer dissatisfaction, whether merited or not.

Lost Packages. Missing packages.

Missed Pick-ups. The total number of requested pick-ups which do not occur.

Missing Proof of Delivery. The number of invoices which fail to include documentation of delivery.

Overgoods. Packages that lack or lose sufficient address information.

Right Day Late Deliveries. Packages delivered after the scheduled time.

Traces. The number of trace requests from customers, which Federal Express in unable to answer.

Wrong Day Late Deliveries. Packages received by the customer at least one day after scheduled time.

Teams Focus On SQI

Federal Express' service goal is 100% failure-free performances. Emphasis is on finding root causes of failure and implementing solutions. This safeguards against repetitive failures.

Quality Action Teams (QAT's), led by a corporate officer, are assigned to each of the SQI areas. It is their responsibility to track and analyze the failure data and identify improvement measures. The team has a four step approach to problem resolution with the acronym, FADE.

1. **Focus:** identify and define the problem
2. **Analyze:** determine root causes or factors
3. **Develop:** discuss possible solutions and their implementation
4. **Execute** plan of attack and monitor results

The purpose of the SQI is to identify and eliminate causes, *not to place blame.* SQI results are evaluated by the EVP and Senior Vice Presidents at Biweekly Senior Executive Meetings.

Fred Smith sees measuring quality as an integral part of Total Quality Management. "The biggest message we can share with other service organizations is that *you must have a mathematical system for measuring quality*. I think we actually have an advantage over some other service companies because we are able to mathematically compute our quality level every day with our SQI's."

BONUS PAY FOR QUALITY PERFORMANCE

The company incorporates management incentive bonuses (Management by Objective, MBO) into the company's annual goal of reduced "actual occurrences." If the company does not meet the goal, *no one* in management receives bonus money for the year, which can constitute as much as 40% of a senior executive's annual salary.

The company's *people* objective is also tied into its MBO incentive program. All management personnel must meet or exceed the corporate People goal in order to qualify to receive any bonus money for the entire fiscal year. The corporate People goal is derived from the Federal Express Leadership Index which reflects employee feedback on specific items in the annual employee survey. The "Leadership Index" (LI) score must be at least as high as the previous year's LI. In addition to meeting People goals, management personnel must also satisfy Service and Profit goals.

What places Federal Express in a World Class Leadership position? We interviewed many executives and employees throughout the company. Here are some accomplishments we observed that puts them on the competitive edge:

- Federal Express tracking system is designed to tell its customers *exactly* where a package is at any time from pick-up through delivery.

- Federal Express creates empowered employees who work in an environment which enables them to make decisions to satisfy customers. Empowered employees also are more willing to investigate alternative solutions to improve internal and external customer service and quality.

- Federal Express understands that employee satisfaction precedes customer satisfaction and has proved motivated employees equals increased quality and profit.

THEY HAVE A DREAM

Senior Executives are highly involved in quality improvement throughout the company. We observed this involvement. Federal Express leadership wants to share its dream with the company. It's a dream or vision of being the premier service company in the world, a company that will set the service standards for everyone else, a company that will set the standard of excellence for its customers to enjoy and its competitors to follow.

FEDERAL EXPRESS DEFINES LEADERSHIP

We were curious as to how Federal Express defined leadership.

"Leaders absolutely have to have three things," Smith explains: "first, a *complete understanding of the mission*; second, *a common set of words;* and third, *an underlying infra-structure*. The most important thing every leader at every level has to show is a strong understanding for the organization's mission. You have to understand what you are trying to do more than any other single thing."

WORLD CLASS LEADERSHIP – A HIGHER STANDARD

"World Class Leaders are distinguished by their commitment to a higher set of standards," Smith explained. "They have a broader mission that transcends immediate business issues. A good example would be Tom Watson who built IBM. Watson obviously made a lot of money, but he truly believed the company had a unique mission. I think it is probably one thing you see in what you call World Class Leadership."

CLEAR MISSION

"You have to define the leadership cadre in a company. If you have 25 people out there and all 25 have a different idea about what you are trying to do and what your values are, you have a real problem on your hands. So that's absolutely number one to understand the mission."

COMMON TALK – COMMON VALUES

The entire Federal Express Management Team has been trained in quality improvement techniques. The training includes customer/supplier alignment and prevention and continuous improvement concepts, along with tools for improving quality, such as cost-benefit analysis, force field analysis, fishbone diagrams and flow charts.

PERSONAL COMMITMENT

Smith acknowledges that he is personally involved with all aspects of the organization and he shares both successes and failures with employees. We heard throughout our interviews that Fred Smith was a "hands-on" leader. Employees were amazed and impressed with his concern and involvement. Smith believes that this type of involvement is essential for employee morale and productivity, as well as to be in an informed and ready position to effectively cope with problems.

Take for example the case of a controversial television exposé. *ABC News* broadcast a news segment on Federal Express during a *20/20* program aired on July 7, 1989, which criticized the manner in which Federal Express handled hazardous materials. In response to the broadcast, Smith published his letter to the president of the American Broadcasting Company in the Federal Express publication *Update.* "I think you will understand that we will continue to resent – bitterly – the unwarranted attack on our company and employees and the unprofessional manner in which it was prepared."

Or take the time a box of scholarship applications shipped from Stuyvesant High School in New York to the Westinghouse Science Talent Search Organization in Washington was accidentally routed to Indianapolis. The Westinghouse staff refused to accept the package since it arrived after the deadline.

But the school's staff didn't give up. They eventually persuaded the Westinghouse staff to accept delivery after Federal Express got involved. Federal Express communicated that the mistake "was ours and not the school's." Smith personally wrote a letter apologizing to the school, "for the anguish you and your students experienced as a result of Federal Express' failure... We fully recognize the importance of every shipment entrusted to us and are aware that many contain items which cannot be measured in monetary terms. Rather, they represent enormous investments of time, talent and labor."

NO "FUDGE TIME" ALLOWED

At least 50% of every waking hour of executives' time is spent on some aspect of quality, planning, assessment and review. Each day at Federal Express begins with an operations meeting focused on problems that surfaced the previous day. An average of ten memo/computer messages from the EVP alone are sent to various trouble spots to facilitate prevention of recurrence of problems.

No "fudge time" is allowed. For example, if a plane is 15 minutes late, the operation must make it up so that no package is late. Any station that has 10 mis-sorts must report the errors and provide prevention plans to the EVP. The Senior Leadership at Federal Express notes that their service quality is only as good as it was the day before; it is recreated every day. "Fix it" actually means *"prevent it"* from happening again, even though the root cause may be beyond the company's control, such as weather, traffic back-ups or customer error.

CLEAR EXPECTATIONS

Federal Express believes in clearly communicating its goals and performance objectives to all employees. Smith provides a compelling rationale for why leadership provides high expectations of employees:

> The ability to manage workforces and to create a workplace which empowers people and continually taps human potential is the challenge before us all. Clearly, the degree to which people *choose* to exert their best effort determines our success in a competitive global economy. Ultimately, their efforts will determine which nations are the international economic engines of the next century. What we expect of our people and what we do to help them achieve our companies' goals is fundamental.

> We expect a lot – people purposefully choosing to do whatever is in their power to assure every customer is satisfied and more. Every day. Without this concentrated effort, attempting a flawless service is really quite futile. At Federal Express, our pursuit of total – 100 percent – customer satisfaction drives every customer contact, whether it's dealing with our billing department, placing a telephone order or tracing a package. The customer must be 100 percent satisfied with the way we've handled it.

> We've worked very hard to create an environment that encourages the highest human performance and we've learned a lot along the way. For example, it became obvious to us that *employee* satisfaction is a prerequisite to *customer* satisfaction.

> We've found that when people understand how their jobs relate to the company's goals, they will do whatever it takes to achieve them. They will exceed our expectations, most likely their own and, more importantly, our customers.

> When people know what is expected of them, understand that outstanding performance is rewarded and *believe* they can make a difference because they will be listened to and are allowed to put their ideas to work, they *will* make a difference.

"A Job Well Done!"

Federal Express has a *lot* of Recognition Programs. It's apparent that the Senior Leadership believes that employee recognition is important.

Senior Management encourages reward systems designed to reinforce positive behaviors leading to quality performance and customer satisfaction. In addition to company-wide awards, each division has its own reward system which ties directly with the corporate goals.

Here are a few of the major awards:

Golden Falcon Award – Flies Like An Eagle

The Golden Falcon Award is the highest honor the company bestows on non-management employees for service above and beyond the call of duty. The award recognizes superior customer service that is typically identified through unsolicited, complimentary letters or calls from customers. The employee receives a gold pin and 10 shares of stock.

Bravo Zulu Award – Above And Beyond

We were told that the Bravo Zulu Award was the most coveted by employees. This award was adapted to Federal Express' culture because of Fred Smith's military experience.

The Bravo Zulu Award provides instant visible recognition for "above and beyond" performance of employees. Adapted from the U.S. Naval Service, the Bravo Zulu flag means "Well done!" The program serves as a reminder for managers to say "thanks" to their employees.

Thousands of Bravo Zulu awards are given monthly by managers to employees. These awards range from theater tickets to dinner gift certificates.

Gone But Not Forgotten – Thanking Terminating Employees

Through formal recognition, Federal Express demonstrates its show of appreciation for a job well done when a dedicated employee voluntarily terminates. This allows the employee to continue to feel pride in past employment and demonstrates to all employees that their contributions are recognized! It creates enormous good will and potential ambassadors.

Federal Express' Mission Statement communicates Leadership's emphasis on customer satisfaction.

Mission Statement

Federal Express is committed to our People – Service – Profit philosophy. We will produce outstanding financial returns by providing totally reliable, competitively superior, global air-ground transportation of high priority goods and documents that require rapid, time-certain delivery. Equally important, positive control of each package will be maintained, using real time electronic tracking and tracing systems. A complete record of each shipment and delivery will be presented with our request for payment. We will be helpful, courteous and professional to each other and the public. We will strive to have a completely satisfied customer at the end of each transaction.

COMMUNICATE TO SURVIVE

Federal Express feels that effective communications influence quality. We asked Smith about the company's emphasis on all forms of internal communication.

"Our internal communication programs are an important component in facilitating the adoption of quality improvement as an integral part of our culture," Smith tells us. "We consider open, candid, two-way communications absolutely essential to achieving our goals. Right from the beginning, we met with our people to share the good news and bad and to answer their questions in a straightforward manner.

"As we saw it, we had no choice. We *had* to communicate to *survive*. As we've grown and become widely dispersed around the globe, our greatest challenge has been to discover ways to keep communication channels open and available to all employees." To facilitate such communication goals, Federal Express uses some high tech applications.

Networks Communicate Values

Federal Express has a number of systems to enable Senior Executives to communicate their quality values and philosophy throughout the organization. Many of the Federal Express internal communication systems are known by an acronym:

COMAT (Company Materials) – a distribution system that moves inner company documents and supplies.

FAXNET (Facsimile Network) – a network of facsimile machines located in Federal Express sites and customer locations.

FEDNET (Federal Express Network) – corporate telephone network used to communicate with internal and external customers.

FXTV (Federal Express Television) – the Federal Express business television network provides real time, live video broadcasts to Federal Express locations throughout the United States and several foreign countries.

FEDERAL EXPRESS VIDEO COMMUNICATION – ON THE AIR WITH FXTV

"Like most companies, we have a variety of employee communication programs," Fred Smith said in a speech he presented at the third annual Quality Excellence Conference in Washington D.C. "Perhaps our most dramatic move has been to deploy one of the largest private television networks in the world – FXTV. FXTV, a $10 million dollar investment, was implemented as an aid to quality deployment with no apparent ROI in dollar value."

Federal Express' FXTV broadcasts daily each previous day's average daily failure points, much like stock market indicators, which translate into the Service Quality Indicators. Company quality success stories are also broadcast daily.

"FXTV has proven invaluable to managing change," Smith says. "At the announcement of any major event or change, we 'go live' as soon as possible, discuss the situation, then open the phone lines to all employees. When I say 'we go live,' I'm referring to myself, our Chief

Operations Officer and any Senior Officer who may be an expert on the subject. Our people don't mince words. They ask a lot of hard hitting questions and we give them straight answers.

"The network was especially effective through such events as our acquisition of Flying Tiger Lines, the announcement of recent cost containment measures and the onset of war in the Gulf. In fact, we were on-the-air live exactly 18 hours after the first air strike on Baghdad. As might be expected, Federal Express Mideast Operation Status and the company's involvement with the military airlift command were hot topics."

In addition to Federal Express' FXTV, *Update*, the monthly employee newsletter, and other such news materials, devote 50% of their space to some aspect of quality improvement.

COMMUNICATING WITH CUSTOMERS, EMPLOYEES, THE PUBLIC – A TOP PRIORITY *AND* A BARGAIN

Although Federal Express' communication activities cost several million dollars a year, they represent a small fraction of the operating budget. Smith believes, "Our communications programs with our customers, shareholders, employees and the general public are an important part of what makes Federal Express service superior to others in the market place.

"Our ability to communicate rapidly and effectively with customers has been a pivotal reason for our phenomenal track record of growth these last 20 years. I believe that the combined cost per package of 61 cents for all sales and marketing efforts for a company approaching eight billion dollars in annual revenues is a bargain. Perhaps more than any other company in the corporate world, we have made communicating with our employees a top priority. But here again, I think the money we spend on this communication is surprisingly affordable. Our annualized cost of communicating with employees is about one and a half cents per package. That includes the cost of all FXTV broadcasts, over 300 publications annually and numerous face-to-face meetings that are supported by our communications professionals."

EXTERNAL CUSTOMER COMMUNICATION

When seen in the same perspective, the cost of external communications is a bargain, too. "We spend a great deal of time communicating with the external public, our shareholders, the media and the communities in which we operate throughout the world," Smith explains.

"Yet our total cost for this communication, including all corporate contributions we make to charitable organizations, is also about one and a half cents per package. Dollar for dollar, I would match the return on these investments with any that we make in the company."

SURVEY – FEEDBACK – ACTION

One of the most powerful management evaluation tools at Federal Express is the management "report card" or Survey-Feedback-Action (SFA) program. We were very impressed with it and judged it to be well-developed and thoroughly deployed. Since it was first introduced in 1979, the SFA program has evolved into a problem-solving tool that identifies and resolves employee concerns. Managers annually receive feedback on whether employees are *truly* satisfied at their work group level. In turn, each manager completes a survey on his work group and manager. In this way, all employees at all levels of the organization are involved in management evaluation. The process provides an overall gauge of employee satisfaction, evaluates management and provides a mechanism for employee concerns.

There are three basic steps in the program:

- Survey: Each spring, U.S. domestic employees complete a one page survey which measures employee satisfaction. In the fall, International employees are surveyed.

- Feedback: Results of the survey are distributed to employees and their work group manager. Concerns and problems are identified and the surveys are discussed.

- Action: Work group employees and the respective manager develop and implement an action plan to resolve any problems or concerns.

The survey instrument consists of a set of carefully developed questions about leadership, the employee's personal identification with Federal Express, reward systems, work group cooperation, job considerations and quality approaches. "Problem areas pop to the surface like corks," says Smith. The survey is a key tool for evaluating how well management is doing.

The first ten questions comprise the Leadership Index which is used to assess subordinates' review of management. Questions such as, "Is my manager willing to listen to my concerns?" or, "Does my manager treat me with respect and dignity?" determine how well a manager is leading his/her work group employees. The company's leadership tenants are taken seriously; managers are expected to demonstrate the leadership traits against which they are being evaluated. MBO plans, which are tied to financial bonuses, incorporate Leadership Index goals to reinforce the importance of employee satisfaction.

Other survey items allow Senior Leadership to identify and resolve problems that extend vertically and horizontally across work groups. For example, in 1990, survey results indicated a decline in employee satisfaction with question 12: "Does upper management let us know what the company is trying to accomplish?" In response to this concern, Smith implemented a quarterly FXTV appearance to field employee questions. He also implemented a monthly employee newsletter which highlights corporate goals. Subsequent survey results indicated increased satisfaction for this item.

Employees we talked with expressed enthusiasm over the SFA process. And why not? SFA provides every employee with the opportunity to share his/her perspective on key management factors. Federal Express has demonstrated the "win-win" results of valuing employee feedback. This underscores Federal Express' philosophy, "Customer Satisfaction begins with employee satisfaction."

FAIR IS FAIR

We feel that Federal Express' Guaranteed Fair Treatment Procedure (GFTP) is one of the most progressive and innovative problem resolution systems in the United States. The GFTP prevents third party intervention between management and employees. The process affirms an employee's right to appeal any issue through a systematic review by progressively higher management levels (manager review, officer review and executive review).

Unlike most corporations where concerns are channeled through the Human Resource Division, Federal Express offers multiple levels of review within the employee's division to ensure fairness. Typical issues include selection for job promotion, fair compensation, discipline and conduct.

The Guaranteed Fair Treatment Procedure (GFTP) process is thought by management to be one of the most important of all Federal Express' processes. It recognizes the importance of each employee as an equal member of the corporate team. Ideally, it removes fear from the workplace. It also provides a unique perspective on the leadership and management capabilities.

EMPLOYEE REVIEW FROM THE TOP

We were told that most of the cases are settled in the first step of this three-step process, but that quite a few get to the top level. Every Tuesday morning, the Chief Executive Officer, Chief Personnel Officer and two other senior officers meet to review grievances. In some cases, they delegate judication to a Board of Review composed of the employee's peers. Both of these boards may overturn management's decisions.

Federal Express senior executives note that taking advantage of this process helps them see that some policies need revision and perhaps others revamped. As an outgrowth of the GFTP, Federal Express changed the attendance policy and accident prevention policy. Even GFTP has been modified from a five step to a three step process.

PEOPLE FIRST

The "acid test" for Federal Express' commitment to employees came when the company discontinued ZapMail – leaving 1300 employees uncertain about their future. ZapMail employees were told that Federal Express would give them comparable jobs within the company. Nobody lost or received decreased pay during this transition.

We heard stories of how jobs were created throughout the company when ZapMail was discontinued. We even heard of how computer programmers and customer service representatives swept floors as a new job responsibility until they were relocated to another division.

The relocation of ZapMail employees proved to be a massive effort. A "match game" of huge proportion was pursued by the corporate personnel division. "I believe there is an important message for you buried in our ZapMail experience," Smith told graduating seniors at Memphis' Rhodes University. "My bet is that history will reflect that the way Federal Express dealt with discontinuing ZapMail may be one of our strongest moments as a company because our commitment to both customers and employees was soundly demonstrated."

During the same period that ZapMail was "zapped," package volume tripled and employees increased from 32,000 in 1985, to over 90,000 by 1990. Federal Express also invested heavily in international expansion. This meant more planes, more people and more acquisitions.

ACTIONS DEMONSTRATE LEADERSHIP COMMITMENT

Baldrige Examiners review a company's commitment to improvement both inside and outside of the organization. This commitment from the top was especially apparent to us throughout our time at Federal Express.

Senior Leadership at Federal Express demonstrated a financial commitment to creating an environment for quality excellence through the following actions:

- *Commitment to meeting customer expectations:* spending $2.9 million annually on market research.
- *Commitment to prevention:* investing 64 million dollars on improved employee training such as interactive video systems and having a staff of 600 training professionals worldwide.
- *Commitment to global communication of quality values:* devoting 50% print space to information about quality within all internal corporate publications; investing ten million dollars in FXTV to communicate quality and information about quality.
- *Commitment to prevention of errors:* devoting 5% of company's total revenue on management and customer information systems.

"OUR CHOSEN PROFESSION CAN'T AFFORD 99%"

It's interesting to note that Federal Express conflicts with Deming's philosophy on Management by Objectives (MBO's). But Federal Express makes it work. "Corporate objectives provide direction for a common effort – so work units, departments, divisions and the corporation as a whole are coordinated and not at cross-purposes," Smith explained. MBO's are developed from the corporate objectives. Thus, quality values are deployed throughout Federal Express from senior executives throughout all levels of employees.

Smith added, "The fact is that almost one percent of our business today translates into *2.5 million failures per year*. Federal Express spends about $800 million annually to undo mis-sorted packages, delayed airplanes, invoice adjustments and other errors. That doesn't even include the lost customers our errors cost us."

PAY FOR PERFORMANCE NOW PLAYING CORPORATE-WIDE

Federal Express puts punch in its goal setting by tying management bonuses directly to its corporate goals. For example, if the manager's goals are not met, no matter how highly productive he or she is in other areas, no bonus is received. Pay for performance is incorporated into job descriptions and performance appraisals at every level. For a courier to receive a bonus every six months, he must maintain excellent levels of customer service and superior ratings on recurrent tests.

OPEN MEETINGS – OPEN MINDED

Company leadership is based on internal customer techniques by emphasizing the inverted pyramid concept in Senior Officers and Directors' meetings. These meetings are televised live to all management globally. The company's quality strategies are reflected in the management by objectives (MBO's) goals.

Capable, effective leadership is an absolute essential factor in deploying corporate goals and quality values throughout Federal Express. "Our corporate success depends upon our ability to fill all management positions with leaders whom people will respect and follow," stresses Smith in the *Manager's Guide*. Over the years, Federal Express has developed a number of programs to strengthen leadership effectiveness and retention, such as the Leadership Institute and the Leadership Evaluation and Awareness Process (LEAP).

LEADERSHIP INSTITUTE – FOR THE BEST

The Leadership Institute was founded in 1984. This Institute constitutes a full week of required management training for all new managers. They're taught quality management, leadership concepts and the company philosophy, People-Service-Profit. Either the CEO or EVP speak to each group.

MANAGERS AS COACHES – MAKE GOOD LEADERS

Federal Express' Senior Management is savvy enough to know that the measure of success for any managerial assignment is its legacy. They believe it is absolutely essential to the future of the company to identify potential individuals with leadership capability. The managers create a mentor relationship with subordinates to prepare future leaders.

In order for employees to be interested in performing the highest standard of customer service, leaders must demonstrate that the company's success level directly correlates to each employee's personal well-being.

The coaching job of a manager also includes those employees who do not have aspirations for management positions.

MANAGERS NEED PEOPLE SKILLS

In the Federal Express definition of management, you not only have to be a good manager of physical resources, but also a good leader of people. *Developing interpersonal skills* is stressed as the first consideration of leadership. The corporate goal is to fill all management positions with leaders that employees will respect and follow. All managers at Federal Express are required to be involved in the Leadership Institute.

The company publishes successful attributes for the Federal Express manager in the *Manager's Guide* . These attributes serve as a guide and reinforcement tool for all leadership levels. In talking to several managers, we were impressed with their knowledge of leadership concepts. Many attributed their vision of leadership to the *Manager's Guide*.

1. Being firm but being scrupulously fair and consistent in the treatment of employees – having no favorites.
2. Delegating authority and encouraging people to use their abilities to the maximum.
3. Being loyal and totally dependable – always doing what you say.
4. Building confidence and setting the example in personal conduct and standards, in demeanor and dress and in one's dedication to the job.
5. Knowing and liking people – treating each as an individual and all with respect, consideration and dignity – having empathy for personal situations and problems.
6. Being available and visible, especially during night shifts, holidays and difficult times.
7. Having the courage to face up to problems and responsibilities, particularly when it means admitting a mistake or offering an apology.
8. Exhibiting a cheerful, energetic, enthusiastic and personable outlook – always controlling emotions as appropriate. Never "crying on the shoulders" of peers or subordinates and never, never failing to filter organizational pressures.
9. Understanding one's self and, similarly, the strengths and weaknesses of each member of the group. Shoring up the former traits while minimizing the latter by recognizing shortcomings and compensating for them.
10. Realizing that every human being makes mistakes, checking that each task or function is accomplished according to standards. The establishment of objective control and measurement capabilities is akey ingredient of successful leadership. Feedback on "how am I doing" is desired by everyone.

How Federal Express Creates New Leaders

We attended an introductory one day class known as LEAP (Leadership Evaluation and Awareness Program) for up and coming managers, "Is Management for Me?" It is open to any employee interested in exploring management possibilities. The class is taught by volunteer managers on Saturdays. The drop out rate is about 16% for the last two years, as candidates discover what management entails.

We were impressed with the class. These volunteer managers serve as instructors and participants. We found it remarkable that managers are so committed to the Federal Express vision of Leadership excellence that they take their own time to develop a new crop of managers.

The participants came from different parts of the organization. The ages were diverse: early 20's to late 40's. Many of the participants had just left the night shift. The commitment and enthusiasm were contagious. The session was powerful and direct. We couldn't believe it! The instructors were actually telling everyone the negatives of becoming a manager! They were trying to talk people *out* of becoming a manager.

The instructors later told us over lunch that it's easier to present the realities of management now than to allow potential managers to stay in the program with false perceptions and fail.

Smith noted, "We take basically good, hard working people who we think are good in management. The people they have been working with get to vote them into management. It's an unusual sort of thing. The most successful military organizations in the history of the world elected their officers, such as the Israeli army and the Confederate army. There is nothing wrong with people electing their managers. It's not typical. It's not the way it's done normally, but there's nothing wrong with it."

An *Employee Leadership Profile* and a *Manager's Focused Recommendation* are also used. Each candidate is coached by a manager for a three to six month period. The candidate is then evaluated on leadership attributes and a written recommendation is made. But the process doesn't conclude there. Another interesting measurement instrument, which is perhaps more frightening to the manager applicant, is the *Peer Assessment Review*. A candidate's co-workers, usually three to 10, will complete confidential assessment forms. These reviews play a major role in future management selection.

The final step for the candidate is to appear before the LEAP Panel Evaluation Team. Candidates must present written and oral arguments to the panel on different leadership venues. The panel assesses all information and either recommends the candidate for a management position or requests that the candidate take six or more months to improve specific skill areas. The LEAP process has been instrumental in reducing the turnover rate of first line managers by 84%.

NINE LEADERSHIP DIMENSIONS

Perhaps the most insightful aspect of the LEAP process occurs when prospective managers complete a self assessment based on nine leadership dimensions. The candidate is asked to provide specific examples of *how* he/she has demonstrated the dimensions and also how he/she envisions using this dimension as a manager at Federal Express. This process forces a candidate to critically examine his/her leadership potential. The nine dimensions include:

Charisma: Makes others proud to be associated with him/her. Instills faith, respect and trust in him/her. Makes everyone around him/her enthusiastic about assignments. Has a special gift of seeing what it is that is really important for subordinates to consider. Transmits a sense of mission to subordinates.

Individual Consideration: Coaches, advises and teaches subordinates who need it. Treats each subordinate individually. Expresses appreciation for a good job. Uses delegation to provide learning opportunities. Lets each subordinate know how he/she is doing. Actively listens and gives indications of listening. Gives newcomers a lot of help.

Intellectual Stimulation: Gets subordinates to use reasoning and evidence rather than unsupported opinion. Enables subordinates to think about old problems in new ways. Communicates ideas that force subordinates to rethink some of their own ideas which they had never questioned before.

Courage: Persists and stands up for his/her ideas even if they are unpopular. Does not give in to group pressures of others' opinions to avoid confrontation. Able and willing to give negative feedback to his/her subordinate or superior. Has confidence in his/her own capability and wants to act independently. Will do what is right for the company and/or subordinates even if it causes personal hardship or sacrifice.

Dependability: Follows through and keeps commitments. Meets deadlines and completes tasks on time. Takes responsibility for actions and accepts responsibility for mistakes. Able to work effectively with little contact with the boss. Keeps boss informed on how things are going, will take bad news to him/her and is not afraid to admit mistakes to boss.

Flexibility: Maintains effectiveness and provides stability while things are changing. Able to see what is critical and function effectively within varying/changing environments. Able to remain calm and objective when confronted with many different situations or responsibilities at the same time. When a lot of issues hit at once, able to handle more than one problem at a time and still focus on the critical things he/she must be concerned about. Able to "change course" when the situation dictates or warrants it.

Integrity: Adheres firmly to a code of business ethics and moral values. Does what is morally and ethically right. Behaves in a manner consistent with corporate climate and professional responsibility. Does not abuse management privileges. Gains and maintains the trust and respect of others. Is a consistent role model demonstrating and supporting corporate policies/procedures, professional ethics and corporate culture.

Judgement: Reaches sound and objective evaluations of alternative courses of action through logical and skillful intellectual discernment and comparison. Puts facts together in a rational and realistic manner to come up with alternative courses of action. Bases assumptions on logic, factual information and consideration of human factors. Knows his/her authority and is careful not to exceed it. Makes use of past experience and information to bring perspective to present decisions.

Respect for Others: Honors and does not belittle the opinions or work of other people regardless of their status or position in the organization. Demonstrates a belief in the value of each individual regardless of their background, etc.

TEAM TALK

We discovered the power of teams for Federal Express.

Federal Express ties quality and participation together with its Quality Action Team Program. This program involves approximately 1,000 teams, known as QAT's. Federal Express found that teams are generally more effective than individuals in solving problems or improving procedures.

"QAT's are deployed to discuss the root causes of hundreds of little problems," Tom Oliver explained, "and to come up with solutions to improve customer service and quality." QAT solutions often result in significant corporate cost savings.

For example, one Quality Action Team in the hub, composed of six college students, came up with a plan to reduce the training time for document sorters, saving over three million dollars per year.

Another team saved a million dollars by working with a new vendor to increase productivity and reduce the cost of the company profit sharing plan.

When Federal Express opened a new international hub in Anchorage, Alaska, a Quality Action Team was immediately charged with streamlining the polar route operation and creating more revenue opportunities. Their results? An average $240,000 per week revenue obtained and an average $65,000 per week cost savings.

FLATTENED ORGANIZATION – DECIDEDLY LEAN

Federal Express' management structure is decidedly lean. This facilitates easier communication to and from employees and customers.

The Federal Express headquarters in Memphis is not located under one roof. Fred Smith and several Senior Leaders are officed in a different building from many of his direct reports. Although this might sound unwieldy, the flattened organization structure that exists in Federal Express lends itself to efficient communication, even though the physical facilities are scattered throughout Memphis.

There are a maximum of five managerial levels in every division. They are:

- Senior Vice President (division)
- Vice President (regional or group)
- Managing Director (department or district)
- Senior Manager (area, unit or station)
- Manager (section or substation)

Through the use of an inverted pyramid, Federal Express graphically illustrates how its organizational structure supports its commitment to the customer. Each level of management supports the next level of management which ultimately supports the front line management.

"A courier's job, for example," says Smith, "is to work directly for the customer. A front-line manager's job is to make the courier's job easier, and her manager's job is to make the front-line manager's job easier, and so on until you get to the executive suite, where the job is to do whatever it takes to help everybody do their best. If you look at the organizational chart in this manner, everyone in the company is the CEO's customer."

BENCHMARKING

"The overall approach at Federal Express is to compare our quality results against our quality goal of a 100% service level for everything we do, and to have 100% customer satisfaction at the end of every transaction. In striving to meet this number one strategic objective of a 100% service level, we benchmark against the passenger airline industry, where less than 100% performance can sometimes lead to disastrous results. In addition, we benchmark against the banking industry, where less than 100% reliability may result in a substantial financial loss to an individual or an organization," says Smith.

Through our interviews, it was acknowledged that Federal Express has been somewhat soft in benchmarking. This was attributed to the fact that Federal Express created its own industry and is innovative in methodology. After winning the Baldrige, Federal Express has encouraged benchmark efforts throughout the various areas of the organization.

THE NEXT CHAPTER IN QUALITY MANAGEMENT

Federal Express openly encourages Senior Leaders and employee experts to speak on different quality issues. In the "Baldrige aftermath," Sally Davenport, Senior Specialist in Public Relations, tracked "over 100 quality speeches a month and that wasn't counting speeches booked through regional and local sales offices."

For Federal Express, quality is a continuous process. "Since we were awarded the Malcolm Baldrige National Quality Award," says Smith, "I have been asked many times if this means we have now achieved the ultimate level of quality. My answer is that the receipt of this award is simply our 'license to practice.' We have recognized since the beginning of this company that the key to our ultimate success would be quality service.

"I believe that another profound series of improvements lie ahead," recognizes Smith. "Our challenge is to find ways to continue delivering the highest quality service at increasingly lower costs. I believe we can do this, and all evidence proves it can be done using these quality management tools. Recently, we achieved our highest recorded daily service level. Just as significantly, on that same day we had our lowest cost per package *ever*. Imagine, the very best service and the lowest cost!"

UPDATE – QUALITY METHODS CONTINUE TO PAY OFF

Federal Express has continued its efforts in quality management by implementing Quality Action Teams. These teams form to address problems that arise within the company, and meet at least until the problem is solved. If needed, the teams continue to make improvements and monitor the situation as Continuous Improvement Teams.

In February, 1993, *The Commercial Appeal*, a Memphis, Tennessee, based newspaper, reported on a quality action team formed to redesign the aircraft maintenance logbooks aboard the jets. Pilots, mechanics and various other employees at Federal Express must use the logbooks, and no one seemed to like the way the forms were written.

Don Eaves, Senior Manager of field line maintenance for Federal Express' mountain region, was a co-leader of the team. He said that the three year old project involved practically any unit in the company that had anything at all to do with the logbooks, including pilots, mechanics, informations systems, hangar maintenance, engine engineering and aircraft records. Even a member of the publishing company for the logbooks was on the team to give advice.

The team has made improvements to the form, making them easier to read and use. The logbooks are now separated from the other logs, like the crew flight log. Everyone seems to like the new logbooks, and any complaints are addressed by the continuous improvement team. Eaves says, "When you're dealing with as many people that have to touch this book... to address their needs, it's well worth the effort."

One change that will be made to the logbooks is the insertion of a box on the form allowing a "yes" or "no" option. This one change will save the company an estimated $23,000 a year, simply because it will save the time of having to check the "yes" entries.

Other quality action teams and continuous improvement teams that have been worth the effort to Federal Express are:

- A personnel division team that saved roughly $175,000 a year by improving the process for employees appealing a denial for a dental, medical or disability benefit claim.
- A central support services division team that saved about $580,000 a year by implementing 16 solutions for reducing the number of mis-sorted packages.
- A marketing and communications division team that saved approximately $50,000 a year by improving the accuracy of publications and speeding up their production.
- A sales and customer services division team working in Mexico that saved an estimated $177,000 a year by working to improve custom clearance and other related processes.

EPILOGUE

Federal Express continues to go forward with its constancy of purpose and relentless drive to set World Class standards for overnight delivery service. This is accomplished through its commitment to quality management... and innovation through employee participation in Quality Action Teams.

Chapter SIX

PIPELINE TO SUCCESS
THE WALLACE COMPANY OVERVIEW

Most of us had never heard of the Wallace Company until it won the Baldrige. Founded in 1942 by C. S. Wallace, Sr., this Houston-based, family-owned business employs nearly 300 "associates." As a distributor of pipe, valves and fittings to the petrochemical industries, Wallace increased its annual sales from $52 million in 1987 to $90 million in 1990 – an increase of 75%! The company has district offices in Texas, Alabama and Louisiana. Wallace's primary distribution area is the Gulf Coast, but it serves the international markets as well.

We entered the lobby and immediately felt a big Texas welcome. Placed on a board in the reception area were our names and titles. We thought, "What a quality organization!" We were impressed to receive that kind of welcome well after a Baldrige site visit.

The Baldrige Award was showcased in the center of the lobby. The receptionist acknowledged that Wallace received numerous visitors and they were in fear many times that the award might tumble over from the crowds. She related as close a call as any occurred just the past week by a group of overly zealous elementary students. We tried not to get too close.

CORE VALUES

From the day C. S. Wallace, Senior founded the Wallace Company, the core values of customer-driven quality, fast response and long-range outlook were an integral part of the business. However, it took a major shake-up in the mid-1980's to cause Senior Leadership to recognize the difference between leadership and management, and the value of the full participation of the workforce in improving quality. This chapter describes the turnaround at this small family business and the core values it embodied of leadership, customer-driven quality, and the full participation of the workforce.

Wallace is a small business with big business values. It is committed to continuous improvement within its work processes and employee development. All employees are involved in meeting the company's quality and performance goals. They are recognized and rewarded for their contributions.

Wallace has a strong commitment to partnering with its suppliers. It conducts World Class benchmarks and shares its experiences with outsiders. The company promotes teams and is dedicated to 100% of its work force being a team member. It uses the Baldrige criteria as a blueprint for continuous improvement, not as a prescription for winning.

DOWNTURN

For the oil industry, the 1970's were euphoric. Sales were brisk and the bottom line was in the black. The distant future looked exceedingly bright for this 30 year old company; however, no one could foresee the black cloud hanging overhead for the troublesome 1980's. By 1985, the Gulf Coast petroleum industry was in a crisis mode. The price of oil plummeted from $44 a barrel to less than $20. The riptide was devastating. This brought construction of oil and chemical refineries practically to a standstill. For the industry, this was the beginning of the end. Two of Wallace's largest competitors filed for Chapter 11 bankruptcy protection. Their huge inventories were sold at bargain basement prices to larger, healthier companies. Wallace quickly discovered that it couldn't compete with the lower prices offered by these surviving companies. It also found itself with over $40 million in inventory, with no one who wanted to buy it.

"We were struggling for survival," remembers John Wallace, former Chief Executive Officer. "To survive, we had to build a new base of business. It was time to change direction and in a hurry. We made the strategic decision to focus on the maintenance and repair side of the business."

PLEDGE TO QUALITY OR "WHAT DO WE DO NOW!"

Wallace recognized that it was imperative to change the way it was doing business. If it couldn't compete in the price arena set by its competitors, then it had to give its customers something more in return.

Trying to recapture its share of the dwindling marketplace made the challenge even more frustrating. The Wallace Company began its desperate search for its point of difference.

It didn't have to search long. In fact, the search for a point of difference *came to Wallace* in the form of one of its customers, the Celanese Chemical Company. At the time, Wallace didn't think it *sounded* like the answer to its problems. It *looked* like just one more problem to add to the growing list Wallace was accumulating. It *smelled* like trouble.

Celanese was involved in a quality movement, spearheaded by one of *its* customers, the Ford Motor Company. As author Bob Waterman describes while working on the "Quality Through People" video, "Ford was getting beaten up in quality by the Japanese. In the mid-80's they launched the Team Taurus program. One of the objectives of that program was, 'Quality is Job One.'

"One of the ways in which all total quality programs are similar is that they all put pressure on their suppliers. Ford put pressure on Celanese. Celanese put pressure on Wallace."

Former President, Sonny Wallace, invited us to a local cafeteria. "In December 1984," he recalls in his East Texas drawl, "Celanese visited Wallace and asked us to embrace quality. It was a simple message... 'to keep this account, you need to make quality a priority.'"

Celanese informed Wallace that it planned to measure, rate and compare all suppliers on their on-time delivery records, complete and accurate shipments and invoice accuracy. The "ideal" supplier would consistently provide 100 percent complete and on-time shipments with zero errors. Celanese explained that it intended to do the majority of its business with a select group of superb wholesalers in return for superb service.

"The Wallace Company embraced Quality as a means of survival," Sonny Wallace continues. "We signed a pledge to improve the quality of our products and services. This pledge was signed by the president, the branch manager, the inside sales representative, the sales manager and the shipping clerk." This total commitment to quality positioned Wallace to confront the downturn in the economy and the rapidly shrinking market.

After pledging to work toward quality, the Senior Executives had only one small problem: **What do we do now!**

As one employee later told Bob Waterman, "It was like facing the devil and he was breathing fire in our face."

HERE'S LIES WALLACE – THE OLD WALLACE

The Wallace Company knew obtaining a total commitment to quality wouldn't be easy, but it was Wallace's only opportunity to hit the downturned economy head-on. The Quality Pledge was posted everywhere – on the company bulletin boards, employee desks and wherever there was an opportunity to remind employees of their mission. "We credit Celanese for helping us to make this commitment to quality," said Wallace. "Today," claims Wallace, "we say that in 1985, Wallace returned to ground zero. An old company died – a new one began." For Wallace, this new beginning helped establish other long-term "partnering" relationships with firms such as Union Carbide Corporation, Monsanto, Hoechst Celanese, Dow Chemical U.S.A., Bechtel, and Brown & Root Braun. In only a few years, Wallace realized it had set itself apart from the competition by setting new standards of service.

THREE PHASES TO QUALITY IMPROVEMENT

Commitment, a three syllable word, is in itself a complete sentence to the never ending process of quality at the Wallace Company. By pledging itself to improve the quality of its products and service to Celanese, the Wallace Company formally stepped into the quality arena.

PHASE ONE – Orientation to Quality

Michael Spiess, former Executive Vice President and General Sales Manager, notes that Wallace's quality journey really evolved through three stages as the company first struggled with what the quality process meant and how to implement it.

The first phase of quality at the Wallace Company was initiated by its pledge to Celanese in 1985 to improve the quality of its products and services. Wallace stumbled during its first year in its attempt to look for waste, improve systems, be a better supplier and to "do it right the first time." For example, Senior Management allocated time to employees to discuss Quality issues. This effort initially took the form of quality circles, but quality circle members were not empowered to implement their decisions, did not have a clear sense of mission and did not document their work. One manager told us that the quality circles became more of a "pass-the-buck, finger-pointing, gripe session."

The finger was often pointed at top management which made most decisions with little regard for employee input. Wallace was structured

the way most companies were – top down management. In such a culture, management does not participate; it commands.

"I remember it well," Michael Spiess asserts. "Back in 1985, we
couldn't call *anyone* leaders. We called managers 'management.' In a
lot of ways, we didn't listen to people. We were too busy *telling* people
what to do. We knew it wasn't right. We knew it didn't work. But
through the quality process, we learned... we earned the right to be
called leaders."

"We really did not know what the quality movement involved,"
notes John Wallace. "We struggled with the quality movement but we
really didn't have that much direction."

PHASE TWO – Quality Training, Analysis, and Planning

In 1987, John Wallace established a quality management steering
committee comprised of Senior Leadership. This committee brought
a local training firm, Sanders & Associates, to assist Senior Leadership
to define needs, design quality systems and implement quality proces-
es.

Sanders conducted an employee needs analysis to check the pulse
the company. The findings shocked Senior Management. They disco-
ered that even though this was a relatively small family-owned bu-
ness, employees didn't trust leadership. They were also afraid of magement, constantly dreading losing their jobs. Wallace knew
situation was critical. It was suffering from customer dilemmas on
outside and employee crises on the inside. Something radical had to
done and fast! Wallace began by creating a tangible list of sha
goals:

- to be the best in the industry
- to learn Quality tools/SPC methods
- to develop on-the-job training
- to challenge old ways of doing things
- to deliver excellence in customer service

To demonstrate its commitment to quality as well as to emplo:
Senior Leadership quickly pointed out that no one would lose
due to quality. "We were selling quality as a way of business fo
future," John Wallace explains.

One of the findings of the assessment was that the company ne
to focus on training and communication. "We recognized that le
ship needed to change," relates John Wallace. "The old *do as*
method had to change to foster participative management. We h

turn from the old traditional approach of using strong directives to encouraging associate input and cooperative efforts. We knew it wasn't going to be easy. Change seldom is."

Senior Leadership responded to training needs with quality awareness training for all employees. It also provided quality sales training for all inside and outside sales staff, Total Quality Management training for all supervisory personnel and quality leadership development for all office and warehouse managers. Total Quality Management was taught based on Deming's 14 points. Sanders & Associates helped the Wallace Company develop project teams led by Statistical Process Control Coordinators. The SPC coordinators underwent an intensive 18-month, 270-hour SPC training program as well as team training. Many associates credit the training experiences as instrumental in breaking down barriers. Senior Management actively participated in every quality training session either as instructors or as participants. John Wallace is adamant, "We wanted to deliver the message, *this is important.*"

And deliver the message they did, at an exacting cost to the company. Senior Leaders became teachers and role models. As Spiess explains, "In the late 1980's, Senior Leadership spent considerable time (over 200 hours) attending training in continuous quality improvement and learning the principles of Dr. W. Edwards Deming, Dr. Joseph Juran, Dr. William Scherkenbach, Dr. Brian Joiner, Dr. Howard Gitlow, Tom Peters and other significant coaches for Quality. Senior Leadership also gained an understanding of distribution inventory management and how to analyze process characteristics of primary job functions."

PHASE THREE – Continuous Quality Improvement

In November 1988, Senior Leadership attended the first "Quest for Excellence" conference in Washington, D.C., which featured the 1988 Malcolm Baldrige Award winners. They returned home wide-eyed and enthusiastic about the Baldrige Award criteria. "Even though we thought we were doing a good job," says Spiess, "it was evident our efforts could be accelerated." In May 1989, at the Supplier Partnerships Workshop hosted by Wallace for over 100 of its suppliers, Wallace Company publicly committed to apply for the Baldrige quality award.

"Quality is the most important issue in America today," says C. S. "Sonny" Wallace, Jr. "It is no longer just the function of the hourly worker, it is the responsibility of every Chief Executive Officer to

STRATEGIC QUALITY PLANNING

Wallace's strategic quality objectives are designed to improve leadership's approaches to total quality improvement and deployment. Wallace breaks its strategic quality planning process into five major components:

1. Quality Business Plan
   This plan is modeled after the seven Baldrige categories. The plan has seven executive summaries with one, two and five year objectives. The action plans for each include continuous quality improvement assessment. The quality business plan is a vision for the future. Associates and suppliers contribute to the planning process by participating in the annual revisions.

2. Quality Strategic Objectives
   These objectives are set annually by management and drive the quality process at Wallace. Company-wide teams are formed to implement each objective or sub-objective.

3. Leadership Retreats
   These planning sessions are held off site to plan, strategize, assess and evaluate long-range quality programs.

4. Quality Improvement Process (QIP) Team
   All teams are empowered with strategic planning, mission statement, advocacy support systems and clear goals.

5. Quality Management Steering Committee
   This committee consists of Senior Management and meets monthly. It is responsible for planning and supervising the overall quality program and integrating its business plans. Out of this plan, Wallace develops the annual list of quality strategic objectives.

QUALITY STRATEGIC OBJECTIVES (QSO)

The quality strategic objectives represent a key component of Wallace's strategic quality planning process. The QSO's are displayed in a dedicated Quality Room, assessable to all associates. These form the centerpiece for Wallace's quality process.

"Senior Management is directly involved in leading the QSO's," says Sonny Wallace. In 1990, the quality process at Wallace was driven by 16 Quality Strategic Objectives:

QSO 1. Leadership development
QSO 2. Quality business plan
QSO 3. On-the-job training
QSO 4. Information analysis
QSO 5. Statistical process control
QSO 6. Quality education
QSO 7. Human resource management
QSO 8. Quality improvement process team involvement
QSO 9. Customer service and satisfaction
QSO 10. Employee reinforcement and incentive plan
QSO 11. Quality Pathfinder bimonthly newsletter
QSO 12. Suggestion system
QSO 13. Internal auditing
QSO 14. Benchmarking (internally and externally)
QSO 15. Vendor quality improvement plan
QSO 16. Community outreach

EMPLOYEE ACCEPTANCE OF QUALITY VALUES

Wallace quickly realized that no matter how committed management might be to quality, it was critical that all of the employees feel the same way. The employees had to feel a personal ownership of the company's commitment to quality. Sanders & Associates worked with Senior Leadership to assess needs, design systems and implement processes. They also elicited input from each employee and produced a video tape which reflected survey results. "The assessment helped us a lot," says Gloria Duncan, Lead SPC Coordinator. "We could be honest and open because we knew our answers were strictly confidential."

On the positive side, the assessment results indicated that employees felt that the company was built on a foundation of integrity and honesty. On the downside, associates popped management's bubble that the company was just one big, happy family. "The difficult news from the needs assessment was that it showed there was fear and mistrust in the company (Training & Development, June 1991)," notes consultant Judy Sanders. "People were worried about whether management was sincere about quality. Some associates said they wouldn't know John Wallace if he walked right by them!"

John and Sonny Wallace recall the assessment as a "humbling experience." As Sonny explains, "You better not think you are on a pedestal because you will get knocked off of it pretty quick."

"I guess nobody likes to hear the *whole* truth," agrees John Wallace. "They gave it to us with both barrels." Michael Spiess understands that the assessment was an essential first step, no matter how dismal the results might be. "We were not as great as we thought we were. But, I think that you have to get to that level of understanding before you can really start building."

As a result of such assessments, the first draft of the Quality Mission Statement was created and circulated to all employees for feedback. The final version reflects input from all. This document is now used in new employee orientation and has been given to all employees, customers and suppliers of the Wallace Company.

MISSION STATEMENT

John Wallace is pleased with the efforts of Senior Management and associates in their efforts to create Wallace's mission statement. "We wanted ownership with our associates in our mission statement. We wanted 100% involvement and their values reflected in the statement. It took three drafts and six months to complete. They wrote it and we all owned it."

COMMUNICATING VALUES

One of the areas in the assessment identified as a weakness was company communications, an integral part of the dissemination of company values. Wallace now uses a variety of communications systems for sharing Quality values. These include:

- branch site visits by Senior Leadership
- a bimonthly newsletter
- company meetings and teleconferences
- individual branch bulletin boards where SPC data, the mission statement, and letters of recommendation are posted
- company wide quality planning/deployment retreats
- on-site SPC coordinators
- total employee involvement in the Quality Improvement Process team network.

Wallace created 110 quality teams, each *empowered* to accomplish its mission. As Bob Waterman analyzes, "Bureaucracies specialize in lines, charts and tall hierarchies. The problem is that most improvement ideas happen across functions, across normal bureaucratic lines. And that means you have to get out of your little box and work with others. And that means teamwork."

SUCCESS FACTORS FOR QUALITY VALUES

Michael Spiess directly attributes the success of the Wallace Company to four factors:

PEOPLE – Trained, empowered, involved – a sense of belonging – What I do today makes a difference.

FAITH – That things can and will get better. Each of us can make a difference. Each of us can make our own future. That we can adopt and change quickly with the environment.

VISION – Always look ahead. Take pro-active steps to make your vision come true.

PROGRAM – The Malcolm Baldrige National Quality Award is our blueprint for success.

INTERNAL COMMUNICATION

As Michael Spiess sees it, "The ultimate communications vehicle for Wallace is the Quality Mission Statement, developed with input from all associates."

In addition to the previously mentioned methods of communicating within the company, Wallace further employs an *open door policy*. "Since the company's founding in 1942, Wallace has maintained an executive open door policy," Wallace explains. "Because we are a small company, any employee in the company can call any senior executive with a problem, a concern or a 'quality win.' Both Wallace brothers related that the Baldrige examiners were impressed with how comfortable associates were with two-way company communication.

"Because all employees participated in Dr. Deming's red bead exercise, employees share a popular vehicle for bringing problems related to common cause variation to the attention of top leadership. For example, an associate may say to me, 'I just found a red bead in the order entry process.' "

AUTHORS' NOTE:

In the famous red bead experiment, Dr. Deming directs volunteers ("willing workers") to follow specific procedures for dipping a paddle with 50 bead-sized holes into a box containing 800 red and 3200 white beads. The "willing workers" are directed to dip the paddle into the box. The workers are inspected for the number of red beads they pull out. The workers' job is to produce white beads. The work standard is 50 and the customer will not accept red beads. Red beads represent a problem or defect. Despite the workers' best efforts, they continue to produce red beads.

The point of the experiment is that unless the system itself is changed, the workers will continue to produce red beads. The experiment underscores the fact that numerical goals are often meaningless; rigid procedures do not necessarily produce quality and that inspection does not eliminate defects. The workers were part of a system that was beyond their control. It was the system, not their skills, that determined performance. The moral of the parable is that only management has the ability to change the system, and hence the variability of the system.

EXTERNAL COMMUNICATION

Even prior to winning the Baldrige Award, Senior Executive Management was committed to taking the message of continuous quality improvement outside the company to suppliers, customers, professional groups and schools and community organizations.

Following the award, Wallace further increased its quality communications to outside groups by hosting "Visitor Days" twice a month with a one and a half hour tour of Wallace facilities.

ASSOCIATES SPEAK: MANAGEMENT LISTENS

As a follow-up to the 1987 needs assessment, Wallace conducted a mini-survey in early Spring 1990. The goal was to determine whether the company had made progress in instilling the value of quality since the 1987 needs assessment. "The data," says John Wallace, "reinforced management's perception that continuous quality improvement is a high value at the Wallace Company."

In 1990, Wallace completed another goal in its quality movement – the training of all employees in the study of cycle reduction criteria.

The company additionally began the study of self-auditing in terms of total defect per unit (TDU's) applied to service. As part of the training, quality successes and quality problems are discussed and analyzed.

Recognition plays an important part in the training sessions. Associates are recognized for their participation in teams and training. During biweekly teleconferences, team quality wins and suggestions are cited. The results are then published in the company newsletter. John Wallace also sends congratulatory letters to associates' homes. Teams are rewarded with dinners and picnics. As a result of benchmarking Milliken's recognition program, Wallace instituted "sharing days" to help build teamwork and participation.

John Wallace told us that he felt that the associates operated as a family unit with a kinship of shared quality values.

MANAGEMENT INVOLVEMENT THROUGH TRAINING

We were amazed by the number of training hours averaged by each associate. This is definitely "Best in Class" for a small company. Prior to winning the Baldrige, over 9,000 hours of quality management training was dedicated by the Wallace Company. From 1987-1990, branch managers participated in 4200 hours and department managers received 5100 hours.

Branch and department managers are part of key teams such as the QIP Coordinating Board. They are responsible for achieving specific quality strategic objectives. They also attend monthly assessment meetings and QSO retreats.

MANAGEMENT TRAINING

Each member of the Senior Executive Leadership team received over 200 hours of quality training through seminars taught by such major quality gurus as Dr. W. Edwards Deming, Dr. Arnold Feigenbaum, Dr. Joseph Juran, Dr. William Scherkenbach and Dr. Brian Joiner, among others.

ASSOCIATE TRAINING

"Over the last few years, we've invested over $700,000 and 19,000 hours of training and education in our most important resource — our people," assesses John Wallace. "Senior Leadership is dedicated to providing education and training to each and every associate. The policy at Wallace Company is that no training will be presented, whether quality training or on-the-job training, without at least one member of Senior Management present to reinforce the message. This is important.

"We took all the training that was offered to any of our associates. We want associates to know that this is *real* important and not just the flavor of the month. We make an effort to be visible and to let our associates know that we are truly committed. And this ties back to quality leadership. Leadership cannot be delegated. Leaders must lead. They can't just be cheerleaders."

Sonny Wallace is in total agreement. "John and I travel to each branch to talk about quality. We want associates to understand that quality is essential. That's why we were giving up our day to fly over to Mobile or Louisiana to our branch locations and spend the day in training with associates. And during the training, we always participated on the teams, just like everybody else."

Quality training at Wallace includes a varied and wide range of topics such as: quality awareness, statistical process control, sales, customer service, coaching, leadership, SPC problem solving, communication/motivation skills, data collection skills, product knowledge, cycle time reduction, failure mode and effects analysis, process capability, supplier certification, benchmarking, quality business planning and information analysis.

The Wallace Company pledges its support to enable all employees to:

- Perform their jobs at consistent Quality levels.
- Understand and meet the needs of our customers, both internal and external.
- Utilize the tools of Statistical Process Control.
- Work for continuous improvement of all systems and processes.
- Manage and train others for competency and quality according tothe philosophy and precepts of this document.
- Master and model the principles of quality leadership.
- Respond to all within the Wallace community and within the community at large with honesty, integrity and a standard of excellence.

Employee response to such training is impressive. "Wallace Company showed a 700 percent increase in associate participation between 1985 and 1990, a 37-fold increase in time allocated to quality activities and a 12-fold increase in innovative projects resulting from quality teams," says Spiess.

SUPPLIER TRAINING

John Wallace acknowledges that Wallace's supplier training is a major part of its quality effort that is unique to its industry. During 1989, 15 of Wallace's suppliers started quality processes because of Wallace's influence.

EMPOWERING EMPLOYEES

"The opportunity to watch the personal development of all our 280 associates has to be the biggest win for me in the whole quality process," says Sonny Wallace. "Quality opened the gates of our corral. We wanted to create a corporate culture which tears down barriers to individual excellence and banishes fear of taking extraordinary actions to achieve extraordinary standards of quality.

"Our goal was to unleash the vast potential of every member of our company to pursue quality," he adds, "so that reaching previously unattainable goals becomes a daily occurrence. Seeing the results of challenged, trained and stretched minds is my most gratifying experience.

"Our associates are full stakeholders and are fully empowered to achieve quality in every aspect of their jobs. But you must do more than simply tell your associates that you're fully empowering them to achieve quality. You must back it up. And sometimes your organization's leadership will be tested. We are tested continuously."

EXAMPLES OF EMPOWERMENT

An example that demonstrates employee empowerment is the *Case of Shipped Flanges*. As John Wallace explains, "A shipment of flanges was purchased from an overseas manufacturer for delivery to a Wallace customer. On the boat trip over, the shrink wrap on the carton tore allowing sea water to rust the outside of the flanges. The Wallace associate receiving the flanges refused to accept the shipment.

"The damage was more cosmetic than anything else, but the associate felt that Wallace shouldn't deliver it to the customer. He came into my office and said, 'I wanted to let you know that I just refused the shipment you were looking forward to receiving.' Not only was the associate being quality conscious, but he was giving his new empowerment a test spin.

"We stood behind his decision and purchased flanges at higher domestic prices in order to keep the delivery commitment to the customer. To be honest, the credibility our quality process gained in the eyes of our associates more than made up for the money we lost on the order."

Michael Spiess laughs about Wallace's early attempts to empower employees because it represented such a contrast from the previous 40 years of top-down management structure. "The culture shock was major. The first time we walked out in the warehouse and asked an employee about his opinion about a problem, everyone thought we had smelled a little too much pipe sealant! We weren't unlike other companies though. We had never operated like that. We moved from a Lone Ranger management style to an inclusive, participatory style."

TEAMS

The evolution of associate involvement has matured from the quality circles in 1985 to a fully empowered quality process team network throughout the company. We observed numerous teams throughout the Wallace plant. Teams appeared to drive *everything*. We were impressed with what seemed to be a total involvement of the work force and the attention to detail through team involvement. For example, quality improvement process teams solve SPC problems, streamline job processes, monitor cycle time reduction, study failure mode and effects analysis and improve processes in all divisions.

Throughout the Wallace Company, interdepartmental teams are used. Frequently, these teams bring internal customers and suppliers together to resolve problems. One result of such a team meeting was the creation of the "sales assistant" concept. The inside sales and customer service teams got together and identified the problem along with a workable solution.

Branch managers consistently work together on teams. Independent of Senior Leadership, ten branch managers met and elected five representatives to the recognition and reinforcement team. John Wallace sees the most effective strategy implemented to promote cooperation among branch managers at the Quality Planning Retreats. These working retreats enable the managers to plan quality improvement together, to get to know each other as individuals working towards the same overall goals for quality.

Wallace involves three management levels in using quality principles to supervise others. The organizational structure includes Senior Leadership, branch managers, department managers, and exempt and non-exempt staff. A major goal for Wallace is to stay close to associates. Additionally, we noted that a flattened organization allows a small company like Wallace to reduce cycle time in areas such as distribution and customer service.

BENCHMARKING – "COPYING THE BEST"

The Wallace Company employs benchmarking extensively in its quality planning. "Most benchmarking has involved the chemical and petrochemical industries, which comprise nearly 85 percent of our customer base," says Michael Spiess. "We have also benchmarked previous Malcolm Baldrige winners such as Milliken Company."

We thought that benchmarking was a Wallace strength. During our lunch at the local Houston cafeteria, Sonny expounded some interesting benchmarking rationale: "My company car is a Cadillac. Why? Besides the fact that the dealership gave us a deal we couldn't refuse, Cadillac is a quality company and a fellow winner of the Baldrige Award. We support quality products at Wallace. If we want to be the best and be known as a quality company, we must benchmark the very best.

"There is no point in re-inventing the wheel. If somebody else has a good program or way of doing things, we'd like to learn from them. In quality terms it is called benchmarking. *To me, well, I call it copying the best of a company.*"

LONG TERM COMMITMENT TO IMPROVEMENT

Wallace's readiness to focus on long-term gains rather than short-term profits is apparent in its strategic planning:

- opening of two new branch offices
- major refurbishing to branch facilities
- purchase of an IBM 9370-90 mainframe
- commitment of more than $700,000 to employee training
- allocation of a minimum of one day per week per branch (five at corporate) for SPC activities
- shared cost of suppliers at Quality training seminars
- replacement of 90% of the truck fleet
- pro-employee change in the car leasing policy

SUPPLIER AND CUSTOMER PARTNERING

Quality partnering is the relationship involving close cooperation between two organizations working toward common goals. It is an attitude of "united we stand or divided we fall." Partnering requires a paradigm shift in thinking from adversaries to team members.

John Wallace further explains, "The perception of most companies is that they are an island unto themselves. But the real infrastructure is like an iceberg with the bulk of it below the surface. That's the way the relationships are! The strength of our company depends on our suppliers and our customers."

CUSTOMERS AS DRIVING FORCE

"In the very early stages of our quality process, it became quite evident that customers would be the major driving force in its movement. From the beginning, customers like Celanese made it clear that the distributors of the future would need to be accountable for the quality of the material they furnish. We determined," notes Wallace, "that this could be accomplished by:

1. cutting down the number of manufacturers from over 2,000 to a little over 325.
2. breaking down the arm's length relationship, by opening up the line of communication to where there was a mutual understanding of what all sides needed to satisfy our customer.
3. assisting our suppliers by giving them the tools necessary to achieve the new requirements."

To educate both customers and suppliers, Wallace developed a concept known as a Tri-level task force. This task force consisted of suppliers, customers and Wallace representatives who worked together to identify mutually agreeable criteria for certifying suppliers. "We all sat down at the same table to determine customer needs and how we could all accommodate them. We needed to get input from all three groups to obtain commitment," Wallace affirms.

SUPPLIER CERTIFICATION

Wallace benchmarked Monsanto Chemical Company, obtained a copy of Monsanto's supplier certification program and held many interviews with Monsanto's customers. After several months, Wallace began a pilot certification program. "We feel like we have a solid, well thought out certification program which we now use with our suppliers. To fully meet *our* requirements will take one to two years, so we are working with our suppliers to bring them up to this level," says

John Wallace. The Wallace Company realizes the important thing is to give its suppliers the tools and the assistance-partnershipping. In the future, Wallace will be able to show statistically that its suppliers meet or exceed customer specifications.

Wallace is World Class in working with its supplier network. After all, Wallace was forced to improve its own quality by one of *its* major customers. Now, supplier quality development is a Wallace strength.

BALDRIGE AS THE ROAD MAP TO QUALITY

Why do companies even bother with the Malcolm Baldrige criteria?

"I think it is important to put quality and the Baldrige Award criteria in perspective," answers Spiess. "From the outset, the Baldrige served as a road map to quality for Wallace. It proved to be an excellent guide, not because we won the award, but because it led us toward our quality goals. We were committed to achieving quality before applying for the Baldrige Award, but the application provided us with the breakthrough to comprehensive quality in all aspects of our business.

"It is true that the Baldrige Award is not a guaranteed remedy for every malady confronting business; neither is quality itself a guarantee of success. Rather, quality is the crucial dimension of corporate culture that breeds the best solutions to any business challenges. Quality makes success possible."

Bob Waterman offers this analysis: "Initially, Wallace studied quality gurus and tried a variety of training programs. But Wallace had no guidelines. They had bits and pieces of the quality process, and they were learning a lot, but they had no idea how to put it together. Then they discovered the Baldrige criteria. Suddenly they knew how to put all the pieces in place.

"The Baldrige Award is criticized for failing to be something that it was never intended to be: a panacea. But it should be respected for what it is: a symbol of the rediscovery of quality in American business."

That pride is reflected in Senior Management's reflections on Baldrige. "I know I share the pride of everybody at Wallace when I tell you how exciting it is to be part of the Baldrige process and America's rediscovery of the value of quality," John Wallace told us. "We have learned about the power of team decision making; empowering your associates; selling on the basis of cost in lieu of price; the advantages of single sourcing and the mutual benefits of partnering."

"The enthusiasm for the Baldrige Award is enthusiasm for quality," adds Spiess. "Whether the Baldrige Award stimulated that enthusiasm or merely provided it a focal point is unimportant. What counts is the commitment to quality that the Baldrige Award represents."

The Baldrige criteria provided measurement guidelines for Wallace. The purpose was to establish a company lifestyle that continues after the thrill of victory is past. That is a message Wallace sends to other Baldrige applicants – *view the application process as a road map for quality.*

"To develop a truly meaningful approach to quality, all organizations must assess themselves against a World Class standard," Spiess emphasizes. "Baldrige is that standard. Baldrige causes a total focus within an organization. Thus, one learns more about that organization than ever thought possible. Today, the Baldrige criteria serves as a road map to quality for many companies and organizations, and it has proven to be an excellent guide in that it leads those organizations and companies toward their quality goals.

"A misguided Baldrige Award applicant who confuses winning with quality is not likely to win, and certainly will not derive the benefits of true quality. Employers, customers, suppliers, and competitors recognize quality when they see it."

ROADBLOCK OR OPPORTUNITY FOR IMPROVEMENT?

So, where do you start on the road to quality and to compete in Baldrige? "To be frank, it will take a company three to five years to be ready to submit an application," admits Sonny Wallace. "We first recommend that you obtain an application and score yourself. And grade yourself harshly. Be brutal. We were, and it helped toughen us and focus us on the task. An organization must score at least in the 700 + range to merit a site visit.

"We wrote our own application. It took six weeks and included eight associates on the team. We committed to go for the Baldrige and publicly stated this at a supplier workshop in May of 1989. We looked at the Baldrige application and liked it so much we used it as a road map to quality."

Wallace divided into teams to address each section of the application. As one Senior Officer remembers, "It was particularly interesting to see what we thought was pertinent in 1989 and how our perspective changed in one year."

Wallace began the actual writing process six weeks *prior* to the deadline and had 45 minutes to spare when Mike Spiess took the application to Federal Express. "We thought six weeks was plenty of time because we did a lot of preliminary work on the application prior to the actual writing," Wallace laughs.

TEAMS HELP WRITE APPLICATION

So, with the previous year's application as a reference and teams as the structure, work on the winning application began. "All teams made written suggestions," Wallace explains, "as to what they thought best answered the questions asked. A particular emphasis was given to what each team thought most directly impacted each question. This process took two days away from the office.

"What I'm emphasizing here is that we had over 30 associates trying to come up with good answers – answers that addressed the questions with factual examples, not anecdotal examples."

The next team to move into action was the Writing Team (approximately eight people). It spent a week in retreat at April Sound, complete with computers, fax machines and notes from the prior retreat. "There was a lot of writing, critiquing and rewriting." Explains Wallace, "We thought we could get the job done in a week, but a week was not enough."

The team approach paid off. According to Wallace, "I think that one of our most important strategies in writing our application was getting consensus on our answers. While we tried to include evidence that most directly met the criteria, sometimes we compromised by cross referencing one piece of pertinent information to more than one section."

The first "final draft" was 65 pages. Since the maximum allowed was 50 pages, Wallace had the additional problem of what to delete. The last hurdle the group faced was whether to print the charts and graphs in color. There wasn't a color printer available in the Houston area. One had to be flown in from Atlanta.

DOCUMENTATION – MONUMENTAL EFFORT

After Wallace submitted its application, it discovered an oversight. Documentation. Wallace explains, "While we had concentrated on the writing, we hadn't done a good job of retaining our documentation. So, after we submitted our application, we decided we needed to collect documentation and store it in a form that was very accessible to the examiners if we were selected for a site visit.

"This was a monumental effort. We ended up with three six foot, five-drawer file cabinets. We documented by section, by subsection, by paragraph and by sentence. We left no statement undocumented. Obviously, we are happy with the results."

WORTH ALL THE EFFORT

"The other day, a colleague asked me if winning the Baldrige was worth all the effort," said Sonny Wallace. "I thought about people's dreams in life. We all have them. Both professional and personal ones. But often times, that is what they remain, just dreams. Rarely do you get the opportunity to live a dream. Well, at Wallace, 270 people worked hard and realized one of their dreams. And we'll cherish it forever. Yes, winning the Baldrige is definitely worth it.

"My message is: **Small companies can do it.** It does take some extra time and effort. It is affordable. You can get a lot of insights from your associates in the process. It's another example of teams pulling together."

STILL CLIMBING THE MOUNTAIN

A frequent question to Baldrige winners is, "How does your company sustain the momentum that the Baldrige award helped foster?" Wallace has no trouble with an answer. "The answer is easier than you might expect. When your entire organization realizes that the Baldrige award is a critically important part of your quality base, then it becomes abundantly clear that the sky's the limit in terms of continuous improvement and achievement."

"Quality is an incredibly personal business to our associates," said Wallace. "By making quality a personal driving force in job performance, our associates keep the Baldrige honor in perspective and continue to stretch themselves to attain even greater goals. Even though we won the Baldrige award, we're not to the top of the mountain yet."

BALDRIGE AFTERMATH: DID BALDRIGE CAUSE FINANCIAL PROBLEMS?

Less than a year after winning the Baldrige award, the *Houston Chronicle* reported that Wallace was in financial trouble because its executives spent too much time delivering speeches across the country and giving plant tours. Gail Cooper was hired as a financial troubleshooter to help solve Wallace's financial woes. His assessment: the interruption and diversion of management over the span of time required to win the Baldrige Award may have been a contributing factor to the financial problems. However, former vice-president Michael Spiess told us that "winning the 1990 Malcolm Baldrige National Quality Award had nothing to do with the financial situation which surfaced in the summer of 1991." Spiess told us that the factors which contributed to the financial crisis included:

- The company's capital base eroded during the depression which hit the Gulf Coast during the mid-1980's. There were no more deep pockets with which to provide additional capital.

- The economic recession of 1991 has been felt by the industry, and Wallace has not been spared. The company's sales revenues began a downward trend at the close of fiscal year 1990-1991 because of that recession.

- The financial difficulties experienced by Wallace's lender, Maryland National Bank, resulted in the bank having to restructure. They sold off their credit card division and withdrew from their asset-based lending activities. The bank was no longer in a position to assist Wallace during this difficult time.

What went astray? John Wallace blames problems on hard times in the petrochemical industry. Wallace's 90 year old father, C. S. Wallace, Sr., who founded The Wallace Company, places the blame on service leaders being distracted by their speaking engagements. John Wallace notes, "You really get caught up in the euphoria. You want to help everyone out."

The Baldrige staff cautioned Wallace not to compete with the large companies in accepting huge numbers of speaking invitations and on-site public tours of the facilities. Wallace noted, "It was our own fault. My fault."

Being a World Class Leader and Baldrige winning CEO doesn't make one infallible. World Class Leadership at Wallace has allowed the company to weather the storm, acknowledge its over zealous attempt to help other companies improve and most importantly, to lead its associates in fulfilling their commitment to total internal and external customer satisfaction.

Business Week (Nov. 30, 1992) reported that John Wallace conceded, "We probably should have been concentrating more on our own business rather than trying to help other people's."

UPDATE – THE WALLACE COMPANY TODAY

Even though the Wallace Company ultimately filed for Chapter 11 protection, it is now pulling itself out of financial ruin. While some say the company has disgraced the Baldrige Award by tarnishing its image, others recognize that the financial troubles of the Wallace Company simply indicate that TQM alone is not enough.

The Wallace Company admitted that it could no longer survive alone, and was purchased by a large fabricator in Louisiana, B.F. Shaw, in August, 1992. CEO John Wallace is happy with the purchase, calling the two companies a "very good fit." He says Wallace will now be "able to offer our customers a complete package – material purchasing and fabrication. We will be financially strong and on an equal footing with our competitors." Wallace hopes the merged companies can learn from each other, creating "the best of both companies." The Wallace Company will maintain a separate identity.

There are rewards for becoming involved in the quality movement, but Wallace knows that involvement alone doesn't ensure success. "We are an example of how there can be external factors that can cause hardship," he said. "But on the other hand, we wouldn't have made it as far as we have without the quality movement."

Chapter
SEVEN

CADILLAC: IN THE DRIVER'S SEAT
CADILLAC MOTOR CAR COMPANY

For many people, owning a Cadillac was like owning a part of the American Dream. Founded in 1902, this division of the General Motors Company produced the car that meant luxury and status. Even the word *Cadillac* eventually became synonymous with the best; "the Cadillac of homes, the Cadillac of washing machines – in fact, Cadillac *was* quality. The Cadillac slogan of the 1930's, "The Standard of the World," says it all.

Cadillac received its first official quality recognition in 1908, when it was awarded the world renowned Dewar Trophy, a prize sponsored annually by the Royal Automobile Club of England to encourage technical progress. It won the Dewar Trophy again in 1912. But that's not the end of the story. Only the beginning of an incredible turn-around.

For several decades, the demand far exceeded the supply for Cadillacs. Those were the days when Cadillac did not really have to worry about quality. There was already a customer for every car made.

But the grandeur that once was associated with the Cadillac name gradually became tarnished through poor craftsmanship and staid management. Market share no longer was solely Cadillac's. The Cadillac legacy was fast becoming only a legend.

CORE VALUES

The founding principles of Cadillac in 1902 were based upon the core values of quality design, continuous improvement and customer-driven quality. For a costly moment in time, Cadillac strayed from its mission, and almost lost sight of these values. This chapter highlights, through example, the core values that enabled Cadillac to regain its leadership in the luxury car market. In particular, this chapter details Cadillac's new focus on core values of employee participation and partnership development and the resulting cultural change that took place in this organization of 10,000 employees, 1600 national dealers, suppliers and the UAW.

THE DOWNTURN

Perhaps one of the most enlightening moments in John Grettenberger's career as the General Manager of the Cadillac Motor Car Division of GM was in 1985, when he realized that something had to change even though he wasn't sure what *it* was. But change it must. Grettenberger succinctly uses a favorite Samuel Johnson quote to explain his own personal motivation:

Nothing heightens a man's senses as the prospect of being hanged in the morning.

"We knew we had to turn the company around. We were losing market share. Our products did not meet customer expectations. In fact, we had downsized our cars to the point that customers told us we had strayed too far from the very cues that made Cadillac a Cadillac."

Its image became blurred and the competition was ready to devour Cadillac's market share.

The Cadillac Senior Executives told us that Cadillac's turnaround began in 1985. Senior Management began a rigorous overhaul of all systems. "Since about 1985," says John Grettenberger, "we have almost *completely* changed the way we engineer, produce and market our products. We implemented new processes and systems to better achieve quality and customer satisfaction. And we're seeing the positive results."

Top management had to do a 180 degree turn in their thinking. They told us that this was a hard transition. Many of the Senior people *didn't know how the average worker thought*. Their top-down level management style was exchanged for a more participative, team-based style. It was in sharp contrast to the traditional approach in which individual departments functioned largely in isolation. This revolutionary approach, called simultaneous engineering (SE), requires teamwork between various job functions. With this new approach, customers are supported by teams involving 700 employees. This includes the suppliers and dealers, who are responsible for defining, engineering and marketing.

The reorganization facilitated a complete transformation of Cadillac, including its processes, products and services. Grettenberger says there were three strategies:

1. *Cultural Change.* A key element was the involvement of all employees in decision making and making things happen. The executive group told us that this involved the union as a partner in helping to drive the change.

2. *Focus on the Customer.* Cadillac's cultural change allowed people to focus on the customer – both the internal and external customer. Internally, teams now consider manufacturing requirements throughout the entire product development process.

   "The voice of the assembler" is also considered much earlier. Externally, the customer is listened to and incorporated into every phase of product development. This is accomplished through a market assurance process, which provides information on customers' input. These needs are then prioritized. Future products and features are tested extensively in vehicle clinics where potential customers rate them against current models from both General Motors and the competition.

3. *Disciplined Approach to Planning.* The cultural change and the constant focus on the customer led to a structured approach to planning for Cadillac which has four features:

   - To actively involve every employee in all business processes.
   - To continually reinforce the mission and long-term strategic objectives throughout the organization.
   - To align the shorter-term business objectives with the goals and action plans developed by every plant and functional staff.
   - To institutionalize continuous improvement of products and services.

THE PAYOFF: RATED #1

Obviously the end results paid off for Cadillac in a big way. From 1986 to 1990, warranty-related costs dropped nearly 30%. During this time period, productivity at the Detroit-Hamtramck Assembly Center increased by 58% and lead time for a completely new model was cut by *40 weeks*. Cadillac was also rated the **number-one** domestic make on J.D. Powers and Associates' Customer Satisfaction Index and Sales Satisfaction Index. Cadillac was back in business.

For many senior managers, the changes and decisions have not always been easy. For Cadillac, the results validate its new direction:

- increased productivity
- improved quality
- greater customer satisfaction
- recaptured market share
- retention of owner base

IF AT FIRST YOU DON'T SUCCEED: BALDRIGE FINALIST 1989

"We didn't make the Malcolm Baldrige National Quality Award in our first try," says Grettenberger, "but we made a great showing as a finalist in the competition. We learned so much about ourselves and our quality emphasis that we were determined to come back stronger than ever – and we did." One thing that did happen in this new company attitude was the return of aggressive leadership. Cadillac reapplied in 1990, more determined than ever.

BALDRIGE – A BOOT STRAP EFFORT

We noted that Cadillac received a lot of criticism for winning the award. There was an outcry from previous Cadillac owners that Cadillac automobiles had problems and did not deserve to be a national winner for quality. There was also criticism that Cadillac over-advertised the award.

Grettenberger is quick to point out the misunderstanding that he believes exists in the mind of the public right now regarding the Baldrige Award. "Does winning the Baldrige mean that Cadillac has cars that are 100% perfect and will never have a failure or a problem? No. It doesn't mean that at all. The Baldrige never claimed to be a product-related award that endorses Brand X. It is a boot strap effort. It is something to help you look at your organization and figure out where it is weak, and then, if you're strong enough, do something to correct it. To me, that is why we got so much out of the first time around, even though we didn't win."

Regarding advertising the award, Cadillac Senior Leadership feels it was equally beneficial to promote the award as much as it promoted Cadillac. It helped heighten the awareness for Baldrige as well as Cadillac.

LEADING VERSUS MANAGING

Grettenberger likes to think of leadership as the opposite of managing. "We try not to manage anymore at Cadillac. But that doesn't mean that we aren't working to achieve a bottom line profit or that we don't have to produce X number of vehicles. But it is a lot easier to get there and to make the best use of the people that are out there in your organization if you are leading them rather than managing them."

Rosetta Riley, former Director of Customer Satisfaction, credits Grettenberger and his executive staff for the Cadillac turnaround. "They were the leaders that drove the turnaround at Cadillac. They were responsible for establishing and communicating the vision, values and methods for achieving excellence at Cadillac."

CUSTOMER FOCUS

Cadillac was starting to see some positive changes happening in the operations side of the business. Cadillac implemented a new product development process known as "Simultaneous Engineering."

It theoretically reversed the traditional method of designing and engineering vehicles. The traditional manufacturing model consists of three steps:

1. Design It
2. Make It
3. Try To Sell It

"Sometimes," says Grettenberger, "you just couldn't sell it. Today, the process begins and ends with a *fourth step* – and that's the customer." Simultaneous engineering embraced that belief – and operationalized it for the company.

RETHINKING: CHANGING THE CULTURE

For any major corporation, recreating an existing corporate culture is not easy. Resistance to change for many people at Cadillac, including Grettenberger, seemed to be the rule rather than the exception.

The goal of a team-based culture requires total commitment and patience from all levels. The entire process takes a lot of hard work and a leap of faith.

Grettenberger recognizes, "My own personal background, and that of my senior managers at the time, was well-grounded in a top-down, management-by-objective (MBO) style of leadership. We weren't necessarily unhappy with the culture that gave us. We simply didn't know any better! Most importantly, we recognized that we were not making the best use of our most important resource, our people."

Grettenberger is quick to point out that changes first had to be made in the leadership. "So we set about to make some changes in the way we approached the business. We knew that we could not ask others to change until we, the leaders, demonstrated a willingness to do so."

Other leaders told us that the real culture change happened within their own minds. They had to re-engineer their own thought process about the way to lead people.

The Quality Plan *Is* the Business Plan

According to R. S. Roberts, former Manufacturing Manager, Cadillac's business plan *is* the quality plan. It is the annual business planning process which defines: (1) what Cadillac is, (2) who its customers are and (3) the quality improvement processes which will be used at Cadillac. Cadillac believes that customer satisfaction is the "master" plan and can only be achieved through people, teamwork and continuous improvement. Its goal is to ensure that Cadillac is once again the "Standard of the World."

During the annual planning process, the executive staff reviews the mission statement and strategic objectives. Then they develop the business objectives for the year.

Grettenberger notes that the business objectives describe the critical areas for advancement. These critical areas were organized under four major points:

1. Quality
2. Competitiveness
3. Disciplined Planning
4. Leadership and People

AGGRESSIVE GOAL SETTING

Every employee at Cadillac is involved in the development of aggressive goals and action plans to support the business objectives. Once the business objectives are identified, approximately six to eight weeks are dedicated by the functional staffs and plant quality councils to work with employees in developing specific goals.

All goals and action plans are then reviewed by the Executive Team. This Executive Staff provides the necessary resources, to remove obstacles and encourage innovation. After final Executive Staff review, the entire Business Plan is communicated to **all** employees in early December.

PARTNERING WITH SUPPLIERS AND DEALERS IN GOAL SETTING

Cadillac includes suppliers as members of the Simultaneous Engineering teams. This allows suppliers to contribute to goals established for future vehicle product programs. In addition, key suppliers are included in "Partners in Excellence" conferences which solicit input into plans for future products.

Cadillac's extensive network of 1600 dealers is involved in the planning process through the National Dealer Council, an advisory board to the Executive Staff.

We interviewed several Cadillac dealerships to determine how effectively Cadillac listened to them. The results were extremely positive. "Cadillac-Detroit listens to the dealers constantly," Ed Morris, President of Bayview Cadillac, Fort Lauderdale, Florida, acknowledges. They've had everything from study groups to advisory councils. They elicit opinions from different dealers *and* their customers. They have listened and our cars are getting better."

Supplier involvement is very strong at Cadillac. This is an area that Baldrige examiners are seeking to find within organizations. Cadillac "partners" with suppliers and involves them in strategic planning processes.

Cadillac uses a satellite system for daily communication with its dealers. This system keeps them in direct and continuous contact with dealers. Notes Morris, "They listen to us and give us complete freedom to satisfy a customer if there's any complaint at all." For example, Carl Sewell, Cadillac dealer in Dallas, Texas, is nationally recognized by such experts as Tom Peters for providing outstanding customer service. His *Ten Commandments for Customer Service* are customer focused and quality based.

CARL SEWELL'S CUSTOMER FOCUS

1. *Bring 'em back alive. Ask customers what they want and give it to them again and again.*

2. *Systems, not smiles. Saying please and thank you doesn't insure that you'll do the job right the first time, every time. Only systems guarantee you that.*

3. *Under-promise, over-deliver. Customers expect you to keep your word. Exceed it.*

4. *When the customer asks, the answer is always yes. Period.*

5. *Fire your inspectors and consumer relations department. Every employee who deals with clients must have the authority to handle complaints.*

6. *No complaints? Something's wrong. Encourage your customers to tell you what you're doing wrong.*

7. *Measure everything. Baseball teams do it. Football teams do it. Basketball teams do it. You should, too.*

8. *Salaries are unfair. Pay people like partners.*

9. *Your mother was right. Show people respect. Be polite. It works.*

10. *Japanese them. Learn how the best really do it; make their systems your own. Then improve them.*

BUILDING QUALITY VALUES

Senior Management recognized that it needed a "vision" that everyone could understand and rally around. Grettenberger says, "Since people support what they help create, we asked all of our employees to participate in developing that vision." Cadillac Senior Leadership produced a 'What's In It For Me?' focus among employees.

"Next, a mission statement was drafted. We invited any employee who wanted to, along with some dealers, suppliers and even some journalists and industry experts to review the drafts and give us feedback. And we made adjustments based upon this input."

The mission statement is designed to focus the organization on customer satisfaction. Senior Management sees the mission statement as the *guiding vision* for everything Cadillac does.

The mission of the Cadillac Motor Car Company is to engineer, produce and market the world's finest automobiles known for uncompromised levels of distinctiveness, comfort, convenience and refined performance. Through its people, who are its strength, Cadillac will continuously improve the quality of its products and services to meet or exceed customer expectations and succeed as a profitable business.

COMMUNICATING VALUES THROUGH THE CASCADING PROCESS

Cadillac's quality values are communicated to employees through its annual business meeting. Perhaps more importantly, the quality values are reinforced through a cascading process by all levels of management. For example, all employees receive a copy of the Divisional Business Plan. Then each staff head and plant manager communicates the quality message to his or her business unit.

Each manager is expected to communicate quality objectives with his or her own work group and to link departmental efforts to company-wide efforts. Managers are trained to reinforce quality values in the Positive Leadership training course.

Cadillac managers are "teachers" of the auto maker's values. They are encouraged by Senior Leadership to spread the 'gospel' of their shared vision.

An executive told us, "It is important to focus on the quality values and the teamwork that is necessary to our success. Through communication, trust and commitment, we are creating an organization that can spot and solve problems for itself rather than covering them up, or waiting until management does it for them."

Cadillac's Executive Staff quickly saw the value of creating a customer-focused environment. This system is designed so that every individual in the organization has the opportunity to add value for the customer.

To assist in the communication of its quality values, Senior Leadership conducts an annual business planning meeting in early December which is telecast to remote plant sites and zone office locations. The senior officers explain the vision, mission and strategic and business objectives and answer employee questions through a toll-free phone line.

DIAGONAL SLICE MEETINGS

Cadillac communicates its quality values through informal meetings with small groups of employees which Senior Leadership call "Diagonal Slice Meetings." The purpose is to openly discuss topics chosen by those employees. Employees either volunteer or are randomly selected. This activity provides access and contact between top management and employees.

We talked to employees who were very excited about the sharing that goes on within their small groups. The Baldrige criteria encourages this type of interacting throughout an organization. Cadillac scored high marks in this area.

"I personally gain knowledge about the needs and concerns of our people through diagonal slice meetings," says Grettenberger, "which I host on a regular basis." These meetings are open to any employee, hourly or salaried.

Usually, the meetings begin with John Grettenberger sharing the latest information on quality or customer satisfaction or sales. But from there, it's an open floor. "They pick the topics," says Grettenberger, "and I try to answer their questions as honestly and completely as I know how."

Another communication activity is Cadillac's quarterly manufacturing forums. They bring together top union and management leadership and the entire executive staff to communicate quality and business information. Some forums include outside speakers such as William Jeanes, editor of *Car and Driver*. According to Grettenberger, Jeanes was so impressed with the apparent cultural change and Cadillac's receptivity to both praise and criticism that he wrote, "A GM division actually *inviting* such a dialogue with writer and editors (in the past) would have been unthinkable. No more. It was a hell of an afternoon!"

"William Jeanes' observation was very gratifying to us," says Grettenberger, "because we have worked hard to open the lines of communication with all of our stockholders, especially our customers."

CUSTOMER RELATIONS

"We used to hide from customers," says Grettenberger. "We didn't want to hear any complaints. All that has now changed." For example, Cadillac has 21 different toll-free telephone numbers for customers and dealers to call. And Cadillac has a dedicated staff of consumer advisors that answer the calls 24 hours a day, 365 days a year.

In fact, many of Cadillac's new employees start out in the consumer relationship center answering calls from customers. "It builds a sensitivity to customer needs and concerns that we need in every aspect of our business," explains Rosetta Riley.

TRADING PLACES

Another way that Senior Leadership reinforces Cadillac's quality values and customer focus is through an activity called *Jeans Day*. Employees told us that they love *Jeans Day*! This is a day when more then 300 engineers and managers, including the entire executive staff, wake up at 4 a.m. in the morning and spend at least a half day working side by side with hourly operators on the assembly line. Everyone puts on his jeans and trades places with hourly operators on the assembly line at the Detroit-Hamtramck Assembly Center.

"It is a real eye-opener," says Grettenberger. "The hourly operators that I work with educate me on their process and how their tasks fit in." According to Riley, *Jeans Day* helps to break down the traditional barriers between hourly workers and management. "People are on a first name basis when working side by side," she says. "And they aren't afraid to come up to you later and tell you what is on their mind."

MANAGERS AS TRAINERS

Senior executives used a cascading approach for several of Cadillac's key training programs, such as:

- Dr. Deming's Methods for Management of Productivity and Quality training
- Leadership Skills training
- Quality Network Leadership training

Cadillac continues to use a cascading training approach to reinforce Senior Leadership's commitment to quality values. The company wants it understood that training is not only considered essential for *employees,* but also for every level of management. Cadillac feels, "In order for us to be effective leaders, we have to know what questions to ask." This commitment to training translated into over 40 hours per employee in the year Cadillac won the Baldrige.

TEAMS, TEAMS AND MORE TEAMS – WHAT A DIFFERENCE!

In order to create an environment in which Cadillac's new product development could succeed, Senior Leadership realized it needed something dramatically different. The big difference between the old system and the new system is *teamwork*. "Radically new," Grettenberger reiterates. Cadillac created and empowered cross-functional teams.

As an example of how this works, each product line is assigned a Vehicle Team to manage the development of new models and improve old ones. The Vehicle Teams work closely with the Vehicle Systems Management Teams to establish product programs. The Vehicle Systems Management Teams develop plans to achieve World Class attributes in the six major vehicle systems. Then, there are the Product Development and Improvement Teams which are responsible for the design and continuous quality improvement of each component of the six major systems.

Cadillac even has teams of hourly employees from the plants visiting Cadillac dealerships to evaluate the quality of the products. Employees on such teams are able to ask customers if they're satisfied with the car *they* helped to build.

Approximately 70 teams involving 750 employees were involved in these simultaneous engineering teams in the past year.

MOMENT OF TRUTH WITH THE UAW – *WHO* IS THE COMPETITION?

Cadillac credits its key success factor in achieving its quality goals as the labor/management cooperation in the quality process. Cadillac has about 7500 hourly employees who are members of the UAW and some 2500 salaried employees.

The working relationship between the UAW and the auto industry has had a less than an amiable history. Top management at Cadillac has worked hard to change that relationship.

"We just couldn't afford a poor relationship with the union anymore," says Grettenberger. "The union couldn't afford it; foreign competition had hurt their image as much as ours."

Cadillac recognized that in order to be successful, it had to have the knowledge, commitment and the trust of all of its hourly workers and the union. But, Cadillac needed a strong working relationship with the UAW in order to have every employee, no matter what their job, ask these questions, "What is my role in quality... and how does my job help satisfy customer needs in the marketplace?"

"We realized that the union is not the enemy," said John Grettenberger. "Management is not the enemy. The *competition* is the enemy. And the *customer is the prize*. Whoever gets that prize also wins profitability and job security. That's the lesson that we've all learned."

CUSTOMER EXPECTATIONS RAISED

It was a tremendous challenge for Cadillac to create the atmosphere that made it a Baldrige contender. It now will prove to be an even greater challenge and opportunity for the corporation's luxury car division to live up to the scrutiny that comes with being a Baldrige standard bearer.

"We're in a fishbowl," Rosetta Riley admits. "We raised expectations and the world is looking at us. We now know that our processes and systems are right. Our product improvement has been tremendous in the past five years, but still there is lots of work to do in order to get our cars to World Class in every respect. And our products are close – that close," she adds, holding thumb and forefinger a centimeter apart.

Since being named a Malcolm Baldrige winner, Cadillac has clearly reveled in the honor. Although competition rules forbid naming entrants, there were news media reports that Ford Motor Company had applied in 1989, and that Honda of America considered a try in 1991. Cadillac's win, obviously, was a coup both for Cadillac and General Motors.

Many critics were surprised that GM's Buick Division did not apply for the Baldrige Award since they have touted quality in all of their national media advertising. Cadillac executives informed us that Buick was not a stand-alone division such as Cadillac. Buick shares with other GM brands.

QUALITY RESULTS

But quality not only helped Cadillac win an award, it also helped Cadillac make money. Quality results began to rise to the surface:

- For the past four years, the independent research firm of J.D. Power and Associates named Cadillac the best domestic nameplate for Customer Satisfaction (in its Customer Satisfaction Index).

- Quality improvements have led to a 30 percent reduction in warranty costs over the last four years.

- Cadillac dealers believe the value of their franchise is increasing, and rate Cadillac as the best in the industry for potential value increase.

EMPLOYEES SPEAK OUT

This story of *one* of Cadillac's 10,000 employees illustrates how dramatic the changes have been. Bill Howey, who celebrated 26 years with GM, calls "the first 20 years terrible, the last six–terrific, unbelievable."

In 1984, Howey left Fleetwood-Fisher Body for Detroit-Hamtramck to join an assortment of employees from a variety of United Auto Workers locals. While a General Assembly worker in pinstriping, Howey began taking classes in teaching group dynamics and from there began studying problem-solving processes. "Many's the night," he says, "that I had what I call 'evening opportunities' – homework."

At Detroit-Hamtramck, initially, there was a major cultural barrier. Employees had come in from three different GM units. "Things weren't done the way they were done in the old plants," Howey says, "and it took a good 18 months for teams to really get their acts together."

By late 1986, Howey went to Detroit-Hamtramck's final process area as a team leader. The cultural change was becoming apparent by this time; Howey was gaining responsibilities. He recalls that it was "like somebody turning the light on."

Now team leader for the World Class Quality Council, a plant liaison group composed of high seniority UAW employees, Howey was privy to some of the feedback when Cadillac first applied for the Baldrige award, secured a site visit, but did not capture the trophy.

"The examiners told us we were putting band-aids on some of our problems – that there had to be more of a plant-customer connection," Howey remembers. "We worked with Rosetta Riley and came up with a program whereby we in the plant began making calls to new owners of Eldorados, Sevilles and Allantes (the Cadillacs built at Detroit-Hamtramck) who had not turned in their Gold Key customer satisfaction surveys after three months of ownership."

Howey says information they learned by talking to the new owners was fed back into the system and "we closed a very important loop."

The loop between employee and customer closed even further when teams of employees began working the auto show circuit, talking to customers and potential customers in a very positive way. Howey was part of an initial group that serviced shows in Detroit, Chicago, Los Angeles and New York.

INNOVATION REQUIRES RISK TAKING AND TRUST

Cadillac is seeking ways to increase creativity and innovation. "We realize that without it, we will not have a competitive advantage," says Mike Sheehan, Comptroller. But innovation requires that employees feel free to take risks. A pre-requisite to risk taking is trust. Risk taking requires that employees trust their leaders to support them in decision making, execution and failure.

Grettenberger agrees that trust is essential to company quality goals. "Without trust, it is impossible to get people to participate. People have to be willing to raise their hands. To speak their minds. To point out problems. And we, as leaders, must communicate that trust to them in a way that says their ideas and opinions are important."

Senior Leadership is obviously trying to develop a confident, "think for yourself" attitude among employees. In order for that to be fostered, Senior Leaders must consistently foster a teamwork culture which raises the value of the individual employee. Several of the UAW employees noted that Cadillac executives were giving them more responsibility in their work assignments. This made them feel more empowered to expand their work into areas that at one time wouldn't be allowed.

SENSE OF PRIDE

Teamwork at Cadillac has generated a sense of pride by employees in their work. One electrician at the Detroit-Hamtramck Assembly Center told us: "People think we smoke cigars and drink beer... that we miss putting the bolts onto every second car that goes by. But today, this plant is nothing like what it used to be. These people like their jobs. They're proud of what they're doing." We heard similar comments several times from employees.

DECISION MAKING PUSHED TO THE LOWEST LEVEL

According to Jim Ballard, Shop Committee Chairman of the United Auto Workers Local 22 at the Clark Street Manufacturing Plant, Cadillac has been successful in pushing the decision making down to the very lowest level in the organization.

He shared with us a story of the Baldrige Examiners site visit. They visited the buffing and polishing operation area to talk with employees. "There was a guy out there buffing and polishing. They just went up to him at random and asked him if they could ask him some questions. So he shut off his machine and took off his mask and they asked him point-blank, 'Who is your customer?' And the guy replied, 'Are you talking about internal or external?' "

SUPPLIERS AND DEALERS AS TEAM MEMBERS AND PARTNERS

In the automotive business, the ability to deliver quality and customer satisfaction is heavily dependent on two other stakeholders – suppliers and dealers. Cadillac knows that in order to be successful, it must consider them as part of the team.

Cadillac shared its strategic plans with its suppliers and dealers and told them simply: "We are committed to developing your capabilities so that you can do a better job of serving Cadillac."

This event completely changed Cadillac's relationship with its suppliers and dealers to a "win – win" outcome. This new relationship allows everyone to focus more on the customer. "After all," says Grettenberger, "it is the customer's satisfaction which *all* of our livelihoods depend upon."

SUPPLIERS

Today, most of the simultaneous engineering teams have supplier representatives as permanent members. Suppliers are included in Cadillac's training programs. Suppliers are even housed in Cadillac facilities.

Cadillac also meets with key suppliers to share future plans and work on product strategies that will yield mutually beneficial results. It recognizes that for a product campaign to be as successful as possible, the supplier can add value in the planning stages. This is a much different philosophy than the earlier adversarial relationship. Baldrige examiners regard this type of partnership with suppliers to be invaluable to help drive the goal of meeting and exceeding customer requirements.

DEALERS

Cadillac dealers are independent business owners who have a franchise agreement with Cadillac. In the past, these dealers helped

Cadillac keep customers, despite product defects. "We tended to view dealers as simply distributors of our products," Grettenberger concedes. "We rarely let them see our new products until they were introduced for sale."

Grettenberger remembers the first Dealer Council he attended as Cadillac's General Manager in 1984. "The atmosphere was 'electric' to say the least. It was clearly an *us vs. them* attitude. Very unproductive. But perhaps justified, since they felt their concerns were not being heard. And their efforts to keep our customers in the face of a lackluster product line were not recognized or appreciated."

And then the change occurred. Cadillac began to listen to the dealers. Cadillac began to treat dealers as *customers* and business *partners*, acting on their suggestions and following through on corporate promises.

Today, the Cadillac Dealer Council meets regularly with top leadership at Cadillac to talk about current products, future products and marketing strategies. Dealers are now part of the process. Cadillac includes each dealer in its market research of future products. It realizes that dealers have a valuable perspective of the customer.

But the communication with dealers doesn't end with top leadership. Dealership service managers now talk to Cadillac's engineers. "We tell them the problems that we are dealing with in our service departments," says Bayview Dealer, Edward Morris. "We even suggest repairs and permanent solutions."

QUALITY DEPLOYED TO DEALERSHIP EMPLOYEES

Employees at Cadillac's dealerships are also actively involved in the quality process and meeting customer needs. Dick Beaver, Manager of Bayview Cadillac in Florida told us this story:

"One of our mechanics was driving up the interstate and there was a lady who was stranded and was standing by her car. He stopped because the car was a Cadillac. In fact, it even had a Bayview Cadillac sticker on the back of the car. He just stopped to see if he could give her some assistance. Fortunately, he was able to get the car started and she soon was on her way again. We did not hear this story from the mechanic. In fact, he never did mention it. A few days later when we told him we had received a thank you letter from this lady, he told us he thought that it was just the right thing to do."

That's the end result of quality: focus on the customer. To motivate employees to be customer-driven to the point of helping stranded customers on the interstate is truly transformational leadership, the ability to cause employees to transcend traditional 9-5 work ethics to focus on satisfying customers' on-going needs.

The following are a few examples of letters from customers to the Bayview Cadillac dealership.

Letter to Edward J. Morris, President, Bayview Cadillac

Dear Mr. Morris:

I would like to take this opportunity to commend your service consultant for the prompt, efficient and courteous service which she provided to me today. But more importantly, she displayed the rare kind of attitude that makes one feel that she is truly happy to be of service.

I bring this to your attention because of the exemplary manner which she has consistently exhibited and I am sure you take pride in knowing that you have employees of this caliber employed at Bayview Cadillac.

Letter to Bayview Cadillac

As a former businessman, occasionally I would receive letters from customers calling my attention to special services given to them by my employees. Needless to say, the letters made my day.

It is my turn to write such a letter. Last month I purchased a used car from Bayview and I must say a few words to express my complete satisfaction in the way I was greeted, the time spent in showing me several cars, accordially (sic), sincere friendly advice and exemplary salesmanship made me feel that I had made a good deal, at the right price and the right place.

I believe he is a great asset to your company. I will be glad to recommend Mr. Edelsberg and your company to others.

Letter to Richard Beaver, General Manager, Bayview Cadillac

Dear Mr. Beaver,

On April 15th, I brought in my 1990 Cadillac to be serviced.

This is a letter of commendation to inform you how pleased I was with your service consultant and for the work done on my car.

I have been a General Motors customer since 1937, and never have I received such excellent service. I rate your service department and consultant the best.

These types of letters are a direct result of the employees exacting the quality beliefs.

CUSTOMERS HAVE FEELINGS, TOO

The thread that runs through quality for Cadillac is *customer satisfaction*. It's the solution to the product problems of previous years. Winning awards is nice, but maintaining a customer base is what dealers strive for. Quality holds the key for product consistency and customer loyalty.

EPILOGUE
A COMPANY CAN COME HOME AGAIN

Cadillac is a customer-driven company that has its sights on regaining market share in luxury automobiles. The company focuses on fast responses to customers through their product development process known as simultaneous engineering.

Cadillac has methodically and meticulously built internal and external partnerships with the UAW, suppliers, dealers and customers. They have built trust and confidence in their products and services that's leading to loyalty.

The Cadillac story is a success story that we all like to hear. They realized that second chances don't always happen, but at this organization they wanted to regain their good name and sterling reputation that had been synonymous with **quality** since the turn of the century.

It didn't just happen.

They did it through a lot of hard work from Senior Management and a focused strategic approach based on Baldrige criteria. Cadillac hit home runs on redefining their dealers as customers, on customer focus, partnering with employees and the UAW, on team building, aggressive goal setting, focused strategic planning and on communicating their corporate values. Simply put, they mainstreamed quality.

Chapter
EIGHT

IBM: A BLUE CHIP RETURN

THE QUALITY FOCUS

Like Cadillac, IBM is a company that built a strong reputation on being a leader in its industry for many years. There were very few challengers able or willing to step into the arena and go the distance against IBM. Perhaps this lack of competition was the greatest single factor that lulled IBM into a false sense of security. The market IBM captured shifted away. New challenges were cropping up everywhere.

Until the mid-1980's, IBM was growing at the same rate as the rest of the industry, including Japanese computer manufacturers. But then, IBM's business slowed down while other computer manufacturers, niche competitors and workstation manufacturers, continued to expand. This increased competition caused long-term repercussions for IBM. A five-year trend analysis compiled in 1990 by Electronic Business showed IBM's revenue growth at 6.4% and net income growth at a *negative* 10.6%. There was definitely trouble in IBM City.

IBM, which had built a reputation based on quality, faced some serious quality challenges. "There had been some changes in the nature of the market and we hadn't changed with them," said former IBM Chairman John Akers. With new technological developments, the definition of quality had changed. Where the quality of a product had once meant its reliability and price/performance, it had come to encompass every aspect of customer satisfaction. This included everything from ease of installation and ease of use to providing complete solutions for the customer.

"And when we speak about quality," said Akers, "we're speaking about the bedrock issue of survival in the global marketplace of the

1990's. Customers throughout the world are demanding higher and higher quality, and companies unable to meet those expectations won't be around as we start the new millennium."

IBM Rochester is clearly a leader in quality at IBM. The division not only won IBM's internal quality award in 1989, but also represented IBM as a Baldrige Award winner in 1990.

IBM Rochester has responsibility for worldwide development and U.S. manufacturing for mid-range computer systems and hard disk storage devices. IBM Rochester represents only two percent of IBM's total workforce, yet it accounts for far more of IBM's total revenues.

As early as the mid-1980's, IBM Rochester had decided to do something about its eroding business. It recognized the need to re-engineer the way it conducted business or there would eventually be no business to worry about. For IBM Rochester, the first step was a hard look at what it represented to the customer. Next, Senior Leadership began by using the Malcolm Baldrige as a self assessment tool. It is an incredible story of how this one location became the "rabbit" for the entire IBM community.

You Lose If You Don't Learn!

IBM Rochester was a Baldrige finalist in 1989, before winning in 1990. "Losing was very good for us," said Larry Osterwise, Rochester Site Manager from 1985 to 1991. "If you go for the Baldrige and lose, you really *don't* lose – you *learn*. Senior Leadership actually debated whether or not to try for the award again in 1990, after we had lost in 1989. We almost didn't. In fact, the vote among my staff was about 10 to one against trying for the award again. Everyone had been so excited and hopeful about our chances in 1989. We were devastated with our loss. And we were concerned about what another loss might do to morale. It taught us some lessons we needed to learn."

Baldrige Gives a Stronger Focus

Osterwise acknowledged, "We have always been interested in the customer and quality at IBM. It was just that we didn't have the focus – the kind of *clarity of vision* to make satisfying the customer and going after total quality really our top priority. *Going after the Baldrige award did that for us. It gave Rochester a goal and a vision.*

"I think we were very good before. But, when we got this vision of total customer satisfaction and the Baldrige award, some extraordinary things happened. We took what we thought was an organized, cohesive, coordinated, well-running site and made it a *platform* for being much greater."

BALDRIGE CRITERIA REINFORCES QUALITY VALUES

What Rochester learned from the Malcolm Baldrige experience helped form their future strategy.

Rochester uses the Malcolm Baldrige criteria as an on-going self assessment tool. All levels of management were involved in the assessment process in the following ways:

- Senior Management was integral to the assessment process and acted as Baldrige "category owners."
- Each category owner had an experienced evaluator or scorer to guide in self assessment.
- An overall "architect" (aka quality guru) ensured consistency and continuity between categories for the assessment.

Before the Baldrige award criteria, the Rochester site had accomplished many innovative quality improvement goals, including their worldwide planning system, customer involvement, cycle time reduction, excellent people management processes and a process management approach. The Baldrige award criteria allowed Rochester to combine the good things they were doing into a management model, and helped them identify things that they needed to do to achieve greater success beyond winning the Baldrige award.

A REAL LOSER? NOT REALLY

Osterwise believed Rochester's chances for winning the Baldrige Award in 1989 were favorable because Rochester had a good product, a good reputation and he felt it was doing a lot of things right. It was somewhat of a shock to him to get the call that Rochester didn't win.

"I decided we just had some work to do. I said to myself and to our team, 'We are going to redouble our efforts; we're going to do much better. Whether we win or not next year doesn't matter. We're going to get better.'

"One of the things about striving for the Baldrige award is that you get feedback. Examiners come in and give you a rigorous examination – they poke around everywhere. Then they tell you how what you are doing stacks up."

VALUE OF BALDRIGE FEEDBACK

When Rochester leaders read the Baldrige feedback report, the senior team knew what Rochester needed to do. IBM learned it was weak in five areas. "We might never have seen them if we hadn't gone for the award," Osterwise reflects.

1. Consistent and Committed Leadership

The first thing the examiners told Rochester was that Senior Leadership was not providing *consistent* leadership.

Osterwise's first response was, "What do you mean we are not providing leadership? That's a pretty rough thing to say. We're leaders. We're doing things. Look at how much we've got going on.

"That was then! Rochester *did* have a lot of things going on. But, what we hadn't realized was that we didn't have much of a focus for what we were doing. We had to bring things into focus. We needed a rifle, not a shotgun."

Osterwise notes, "If we were going to get serious about total customer satisfaction and total quality, the Baldrige people told us that we had better concentrate our fire power where it could do some good. We had to hit the target solid with all the power we had – not just pepper it with buck shot.

"Now, in part, we lost in 1989 because *I* wasn't as committed as I should have been. I wasn't backing up that commitment. I became more committed in 1990, just as lots of other people at IBM became more committed. I think, number one, that's what it takes. *Commitment.*

"We all have our mentors and, in a different sort of way, one of mine is a previous Rochester site manager by the name of Hal Martin. Because of his untimely death, I never actually got to meet Hal. But, I have a letter that he wrote.

"Somebody once asked him what was most important to him. He said, 'I focus on quality and morale because if I do those, everything else follows.' Hal's letter sits right in front of a file I have that I look at the first of each month. I have this letter there so I will see it first thing. That letter is my not so subtle reminder of what leading is all about."

2. Cross-Functional Teams

Baldrige examiners told Rochester in 1989, that Senior Leadership was not as organized or supportive of cross-functional teams as they should have been.

Osterwise explains, "In 1989, we weren't rewarding people for working *together* and solving problems in teams. We weren't walking like we were talking. One of the things we did to correct that was to begin rewarding *team* efforts."

3. Focused Training

A third area that Baldrige Examiners pointed out to Rochester in 1989 concerned training. Osterwise likened pre-1990 training to a college catalog.

"There was a lot of training going on but there wasn't much focus to it. One of the things that the Baldrige criteria suggests is mandatory targeted education.

"In 1990, we did that. We did it in a method of roll down. I educated my people on quality, they educated theirs and so on down through the environment. We put everybody – all 8,100 of our people – managers, key leaders, everybody – through one to two days of intensive quality training."

Osterwise acknowledged, "Now that did a couple of things. First, it demonstrated the buy-in and support of managers. The second thing was that everybody in the class got it – twice. They learned it once and they taught it once."

4. Benchmarking

Rochester learned that it needed to be doing a better job of benchmarking. Osterwise acknowledged, "Everybody tries to learn about their competition. We've done that for as long as I can remember. For example, we knew about Hewlett-Packard and Digital Equipment and Olivetti, Nixdorf, Fujitsu and Hitachi. But we weren't looking *beyond* the competition, finding the best company and learning from them. We know how Fujitsu manufactures their products but they may not be the best in manufacturing. Now we are finding out about John Deere, 3M and Toyota and learning from them."

Rochester began a benchmarking process in earnest that helped model its process after the best in functional areas.

5. Customer Connection

Baldrige examiners pointed out that Rochester was lacking in the connection to the end customer.

"They said, 'You send your stuff off the loading dock, somebody installs it, maintains it, but in some respects you don't care *who*,' " Osterwise relates. "What you manage, measure and follow is what you do here. That doesn't make a company. What makes a company is who sells your stuff in the beginning, who installs it, services it and supports it in the end, plus what you do in the middle, which is design, develop, manufacture and deliver. You don't know when you have a marketing rep or systems engineer talking to a customer and that customer says, 'I don't like the system,' because you don't know that conversation ever happened!

"Consequently, the Baldrige examiners said, 'You can't do anything about satisfying *that* customer's needs or wants.' "

Osterwise revealed that he took exception to this part of the Baldrige feedback report. "We said, 'Wait a minute, you don't understand. We *do* have a lot of data from the field. We have customer partnership advisory councils and focus groups to inform us about our products. We make customer partnership calls 90 days after the system is shipped to ask them how did it go, and do you like it. So, we have a lot of connection.'

"But, the Baldrige examiners said, 'You don't have a 100% closed-loop understanding of all that data.' And, you know something? *They were right!*"

Osterwise and his senior executives took the Baldrige feedback report seriously. They formed a more closed-loop, connective system with their marketing and service representatives. Rochester's manufacturing and development personnel hold quarterly meetings with marketing and service people. Each group listens to customers very carefully.

CHANGING THE CULTURE TO INCLUDE THE CUSTOMER

The IBM Rochester leadership has transformed its culture from reliance on technology-driven processes to *market*-driven processes directly involving suppliers, business partners and customers.

The concept of quality at IBM Rochester is linked directly to the customer. At every step, customers are directly involved in each aspect of the product from design to delivery – through advisory councils, global information systems, trials of prototypes and numerous other feedback mechanisms.

CASCADING LEADERSHIP

Empowered by both John Akers and Stephen Schwartz (at the time General Manager for the IBM business that included Rochester and later IBM Senior Vice President for Market-Driven Quality), Larry Osterwise and his executives created and communicated *their* vision to all employees:

- Customer – The final Arbiter
- Quality – Excellence in Execution
- Products and Services – First with the Best
- People – Enabled, Empowered, Excited, Rewarded

Osterwise and his executives also created a simple but powerful quality policy:

ROCHESTER EXCELLENCE... CUSTOMER SATISFACTION

STRATEGIC SUCCESS FACTORS

IBM Rochester strengthened its strategic quality initiatives by formulating improvement plans based on six critical success factors:

1. improved product and service requirements definition
2. an enhanced product strategy
3. a six-sigma defect elimination strategy
4. further cycle time reductions
5. improved education
6. increased employee involvement and ownership

Each senior manager "owns" one of the six factors and assumes responsibility for plans and implementation.

QUALITY VALUES REFLECTED IN CORPORATE POLICIES

The commitment to traditional quality values is reflected in IBM's Corporate Policy Letters. These policies are expanded into formal quality directives, known as "Corporate Instructions."

Corporate Instructions require continuous improvement of all business processes, product and non-product, to make them more efficient, effective and adaptable. The Rochester site vision and quality policy, developed with employee participation, is based on these IBM corporate directives.

INTEGRATING QUALITY VALUES INTO LEADERSHIP PROCESS

Rochester IBM integrates quality values into its leadership process. Executive leadership is charged with the responsibility of achieving the following:

- *create* an exciting vision and establish policy and management system based on quality values
- *make* quality the foundation of the business
- *communicate* often with inspiration
- *educate* employees
- *foster* ownership and commitment by each employee
- *measure* and continuously improve
- *demonstrate* personal commitment daily

Strong, direct feedback channels are key parts of IBM Rochester's closed-loop system, achieving employee ownership and understanding. This Rochester leadership approach has been adopted by the IBM corporation and is illustrated in the following figure.

PROJECTION OF VALUES

IBM Rochester uses many activities and vehicles for communicating, projecting and reinforcing quality values. These activities include all-employee meetings, regular departmental meetings, senior executive round tables, quality awards and the performance planning, counseling and evaluation process.

The key communication vehicles are *Rochester Today* (daily bulletin board notices), *IBM Rochester News* (a home-delivered monthly newspaper) and *ABS Horizons* (a quarterly newspaper), all of which highlight quality success stories and publicize quality awards.

SPREADING THE QUALITY MESSAGE

To reinforce Rochester's quality goals, Executive Leadership distributes brochures, posters and pocket cards to employees to maintain a constant awareness of its quality policy. Osterwise maintained an open communication policy encouraging all employees to send him direct, on-line messages on any issue. He accepted all messages and personally responded to each one.

Rochester Senior Leaders regularly speak at all management classes, new employee orientations and employee symposiums.

EMPOWERING LEADERS

"We kept the management team," said Schwartz, "all the way down to the first level manager, very much *informed* about what was going on, what the problems were and what the challenges were. We shared information and data with everyone. We did not keep data back at the executive level, which is so common. Managers understood all the problems; they understood the challenges. Managers had the facts, even to the point where we shared financial information, which you normally don't do.

"We were *expecting* a level of productivity that was twice what we had ever done before. It was important that we shared why we thought we could do it, and what each manager's role was. I would say the most important thing I did was to consistently communicate. Whenever there was a problem the team didn't know the answer to, I made sure I got someone from other places in IBM that could help them. We didn't do constant reviews, which was our style in the past. If the team didn't ask for help, we left them alone."

SENIOR LEADER TRAINING

Senior executives at Rochester take an active role in education and training in order to serve as role models for employees. Executives train and coach their teams. Executives attend meetings with customers, suppliers, business partners, competitors and other industry leaders, consultants and educators to learn and become more effective teachers for their employees.

To increase the effectiveness of Rochester Market-Driven Education, a cross-functional team developed the Rochester Management College. The college brings all managers together twice a year, each time for two days.

Osterwise states, "I would say that the management college was one of the most significant things we did. It started out as a management college. We turned it into a leadership college in which we took all of our leaders (managers) off site for two days in the spring and two days in the fall. I helped develop the program, host it and provide leadership."

GETTING THERE: EDUCATION INVESTMENT

All managers receive a minimum of 40 hours of education per year which enhances the quality education they deliver to their teams in quality fundamentals, Baldrige quality guidelines, tools and techniques.

IBM Rochester invests an equivalent of five percent of its payroll in education for its employees. In a single year, about a third of the workforce moved into new positions, and 13 percent were promoted. The leadership at IBM Rochester is providing employees with more focused educational road maps for each employee's individual development.

A theme heard over and over was team-involvement. One of Rochester's critical success factors for team achievement is the ability of its managers to *enable, empower, excite* and *reward* project team members.

Enabled: Education of managers and non-managers ranges from transformational leadership, to manufacturing skills integration (work station ownership).

Rochester's education is supplemented by continuous on-the-job exposure to customers through many initiatives that involve everyone in IBM Rochester.

Many and varied communication vehicles are used to keep everyone abreast of accomplishments and new directions, as well as to seek feedback and identify consensus and issues.

Empowered: Empowerment at IBM Rochester means the creation of an environment for people to take ownership and responsibility of their jobs. In order for empowerment to work, managers must delegate, teamwork must be fostered and employees must be given the tools and guidance to manage their work.

Excited: IBM provides an environment for employee excitement. Employees who are given the tools and freedom to accomplish, and who are rewarded for their efforts will be excited about their job and their company.

Rewarded: Senior Leaders continually recognize employees for their accomplishments through merit pay systems that recognize employee performance.

Rochester executives personally recognize employee contributions to quality in many ways, which include: thank you's, time off and monetary awards. Executives reinforced their commitment to quality by participating in over 200 awards in a year's time, totaling over $1.5 million. For example, Rochester Engineering Lab Director, Keith Slack, awarded $38,500 to an 11 member team that improved a key development process.

Rochester Senior Leadership acknowledges that the ultimate results that validate leadership, morale, employee buy-in and participation in quality improvement is *productivity*. Employee productivity is measured in Rochester by revenue per employee, and that has increased by 35% since 1985.

BRIDGING THE GAP: PROBLEM SOLVING

IBM Rochester involves managers and supervisors as sponsors of improvement teams. Managers are involved in cross-functional teams that investigate root cause analysis of many fact and process problems. Managers become process owners and work closely with customers as members of problem solving teams. The teams are able to determine the root causes of customer problems.

Stephen Schwartz notes, "We pushed authority down very far into the organization. Decisions that used to be made by executives were pushed down to the first level manager and the people themselves. So, we shortened the decision cycles that occurred during a complex system development cycle. We relied heavily on the people to make the right decisions rather than having four or five layers of management checking up on them.

"Instead of lots of management reviews, we used lots of peer reviews. It turned out to be very effective. Peers are a lot more knowledgeable about what the potential solutions for the problems are."

COMPLAINT MANAGEMENT PROCESS

Its goal is straightforward and ambitious. Rochester aspires to achieve the goal of being the World Class Leader in customer satisfaction. The Rochester site has established a complaint management process that links marketing and manufacturing teams. Complaints are received from customers by all levels of management. The complaints are managed by the customer satisfaction management team which works with the IBM branch office nearest the customer.

A Rochester employee is assigned to investigate and understand fully the customer's problem. The problem has to be resolved within two weeks, after which feedback from the problem is documented and reported to the customer satisfaction council. This feedback helps the Rochester site improve in product and service quality.

CUSTOMER FOLLOW-UP PROCESS PROVES HELPFUL

Everyone is involved with a customer partnership "call process" that *thanks* customers for purchasing an IBM product. Team members make the call 90 days after the system is shipped from the Rochester site.

Team members seek the customer's likes and dislikes as well as other comments about the product or service. This information is placed into a data base, analyzed and distributed on a regular basis to engineering, programming, marketing, manufacturing and service teams for evaluation.

MOVING QUALITY PAST THE CORPORATE WALLS

IBM is helping translate quality applications into other arenas in the community. Rochester promotes quality awareness and how successful quality strategies work with outside groups, including community, business, trade schools and government.

"IBM Rochester's community involvement works in conjunction with local organizations such as the education system. It was through the Rochester school district that our organization, Building Equality Together (B.E.T.), began," recounts Roy Bauer, former Director of Market-Driven Quality at IBM Rochester and co-author of *The Silverlake Project*.

TEACH THE TEACHER PROGRAM

The Rochester site is involved in numerous initiatives in a variety of areas such as its *Teach the Teachers* program, visiting scientists and other professional programs. Since 1982, these programs have reached over 3,000 teachers and administrators, as well as countless students.

IBM ROCHESTER – THE QUALITY RABBIT

As a leader, a "quality rabbit," IBM Rochester provides a template from which the IBM Corporation has developed a model for continuous improvement. IBM uses the Baldrige as a self assessment tool to help them achieve long-range quality and market leadership.

MARKET-DRIVEN QUALITY

To implement its overall strategy, IBM developed Market-Driven Quality (MDQ). MDQ is based on benchmarking 50 World Class Leaders, including Rochester, and reflects a collection of measures borrowed or adapted from these companies. Driven by Senior Leadership, MDQ has four dimensions:

A. Quality Actions or Initiatives
B. Business Processes
C. Assessments
D. Support Processes

MDQ includes:

1. *Initiatives*: five points that encompass the Market-Driven principles (definition of market needs, eliminate defects, reduce product cycle time, measure progress and commitment and employee empowerment)
2. *Process Review*: a system for analyzing the flow of business and making changes in opportunity areas
3. *Self Examination*: a method for measurement and comparison of internal/external quality standards
4. *Support Processes*: information processing, education, communication and human resources

As a part of its Market-Driven Strategy, IBM is focusing on several areas of its business which center around the customer:

1. Customer partnerships
2. the *Customer's* business solutions – not just products, not just software – but everything that's part of the business solution for the customer
3. Creating competitive products
4. Competitive business structure

EPILOGUE

After the IBM Rochester site won the Baldrige Award in 1990, its AS/400 mid-range computer continued to lead the market as changes in technology and customers' expectations fundamentally reshaped IBM and the worldwide computer industry. Rochester is not immune. But, just as they led the way on the journey to World Class quality excellence, there is reason to believe the people of Rochester will do so once again as they, and IBM, re-invent their businesses for the 1990's. And, just as the Malcolm Baldrige Quality self assessment has helped Rochester, it is now helping IBM.

Chapter
<u>NINE</u>

A USER FRIENDLY SELF ASSESSMENT

To complete a self assessment using the Baldrige criteria, a company must often times start from the very beginning. The first step is a *commitment* from Senior Leaders to the principles of Total Quality Management.

So just what is Total Quality Management? Total Quality Management is a management philosophy. It involves everyone in the organization in the continuous improvement to meet and exceed current and future customer needs.

The principles, processes and tools of TQM represent a *radical* departure from the conventional way of managing an organization. Some of the differences are outlined below.

CONVENTIONAL MANAGEMENT PHILOSOPHY	TQM MANAGEMENT PHILOSOPHY
• Hierarchical "top-down" decision making	• Network of management, employees, customers, suppliers. Shared decision making, empowerment
• Managers as directing, controlling	• Managers as coaches, facilitators, cheerleaders
• Competition between divisions	• Collaboration and teamwork
• Suppliers selected on basis of cost	• Suppliers selected on basis of quality and certification
• Maintenance and inspection of systems	• Prevention and continuous improvement of systems
• Separation of functions	• Integration of all processes
• Focus on profit, market niche	• Focus on the customer

In layman's language what this simply means is:

CONVENTIONAL MANAGEMENT PHILOSOPHY	TQM MANAGEMENT PHILOSOPHY
• Quality costs time and money	• Quality saves time and money
• Work is a series of actions	• Work is an integrated process
• Quantity is as important as quality	• Without quality, quantity is unneeded
• Hitting the mark 90% most of the time is darn good	• Only 100% works
• Quality is the result of strongerand more specific inspections	• Quality begins at the beginning, not the end
• Suppliers need to be kept off balance	• Supplies are partners
• For quality to happen we need more people	• Quality means training and leading existent staff. More is not always better

Senior Leadership, including the CEO, COO and Senior Vice Presidents, must first be *educated* in the principles of TQM in order to develop a critical mass of leaders committed to the new management philosophy. We recommend several activities that will help Senior Leaders develop an understanding of quality principles:

- Benchmarking the Best Practices
- Learning from the Quality Gurus
- Reading Quality Books and Articles
- Reviewing the Baldrige Criteria

BENCHMARKING THE BEST PRACTICES

Leaders need to know where their companies stand relative to the best practices both within and outside the industry. Visiting organizations recognized for their quality practices stimulates innovation internally and provides a reference for "best in class" practices. Visiting the Baldrige Award winners is an excellent place to begin. As award winners, these organizations are required to share their quality strategies with the public.

LEARNING FROM THE QUALITY GURUS

Ford Motor Company, IBM and Motorola are just a few of the many organizations that have learned "first-hand" from the quality gurus such as Dr. W. Edwards Deming, Dr. J. M. Juran, Phil Crosby or Dr. Myron Tribus. Many other quality consultants are available nationally to work with organizations. In addition, there are many excellent quality seminars offered through professional organizations such as the American Management Association (AMA), the American Society of Quality Control (ASQC) or the American Society for Training and Development (ASTD).

READING QUALITY BOOKS AND ARTICLES

Deming's *Out of the Crisis*, Juran's *Planning for Quality*, or Senge's *The Fifth Discipline: The Art and Practice of the Learning Organization* are just a few of the many excellent books that discuss the foundation principles of quality management. Further references are listed in the Resource Section in the appendix.

REVIEWING THE BALDRIGE CRITERIA

A review of the Baldrige criteria provides an understanding of the core set of quality values and a framework for assessing quality in any organization. Introductory courses on the Baldrige criteria featuring case studies are available through consultants and professional organizations.

THE BEST WAY TO BEGIN
SENIOR LEADERSHIP TRAINING

Plan an off-site *Executive Retreat* to introduce the Baldrige criteria and benefits of its use to Senior Leaders. A quality consultant with expertise in the Baldrige criteria should lead the session. The Baldrige is not prescriptive. It's value is to enable an organization to:

- Conduct an objective analysis of the organization's overall quality management practices
- Establish a baseline of strengths and gaps of the organization's quality management system
- Identify areas for improvement

The Executive Retreat enables Senior Leadership to go through the entire examination process and obtain an understanding and appreciation of the criteria as an assessment tool. Typically, a two-day workshop that includes case studies is sufficient. Use this workshop to actually identify strengths and gaps for the organization in at least one category such as Leadership.

Discuss each category. Ask yourself, "What does it mean to your organization?" Translate the criteria into your industry language, your company's language, even in simplistic, "down home" terms. We recommend that you use the "getting started" activity in the appendix of this book and Fisher's *The Simplified Baldrige Award Organization Assessment* workbook to help.

Focus on the purpose of the Baldrige criteria. It's a road map, a self assessment and internal audit. It provides data for your strategic planning process. It is not a test or a competition. It requires team effort.

TEAM TRAINING

The next step is to determine which Senior Leaders will sponsor each of seven category teams for the internal Baldrige assessment. Each team should have approximately five members that represent different levels throughout the organization.

LEADERSHIP	INFORMATION & ANALYSIS	STRATEGIC QUALITY PLANNING
• CEO, President or Sr. VP (Team Leader)	• VP – MIS (Team Leader)	• VP, Strategic Planning (Team Leader)
• Director of Legal	• Director of MIS	• Director
• Director of PR	• Manager	• Manager
• Manager – Operations	• Supervisor	• Supervisor
• Line Employee	• Line Employee	• Line Employee

Human Resource Development Management Process	Management of Quality	Quality & Operational Results
• VP, Personnel (Team Leader)	• VP, Quality (Team Leader)	• VP, Operations (Team Leader)
• Director	• Director	• Director
• Manager	• Manager	• Manager
• Supervisor	• Supervisor	• Supervisor
• Line Employee	• Line Employee	• Line Employee

Customer Focus & Satisfaction
• VP, Marketing (Team Leader)
• Director
• Manager
• Supervisor
• Line Employee

Each team then receives the same two-day Baldrige assessment training that the Senior Leaders received at the Executive Retreat. The senior executive sponsor for each team co-instructs the training with an experienced Baldrige consultant. Senior Leadership's involvement in training sends a clear message to employees that "this is important."

CERTIFICATION TRAINING

The next step is to have the executive sponsors and all team member go through a two-day certification workshop. This workshop uses the organization itself as the "case study." The workshop allows all teams to work together on a preliminary assessment of the organization. This workshop prepares teams for the actual internal assessment.

Team members look at eight critical factors during the assessment of their organization. Does your company have:

1. A strategic long-range, integrated plan for improving all operations continuously.
2. A system for measuring improvements accurately.
3. A strategic plan based on benchmarks that compare your organization's performance processes with the world's best.
4. A close partnership with suppliers and customers that feeds improvements back into the operation.
5. A deep understanding of customers so that needs can be translated into products and services.
6. A long-lasting relationship with customers, going beyond the delivery of products to include service and ease of maintenance.
7. A focus on preventing mistakes rather than merely correcting them.
8. A commitment to improving quality that runs from the top of the organization to the bottom.

Key Principles

Keeping it simple is a must. Focus on what quality is:

• Quality is identifying and meeting customer requirements.
• Quality "standard" is service and products free from mistakes.
• Quality is achievable through prevention, not inspection.
• Quality and measurement go hand in hand. Measurements identify areas of opportunity to keep "raising the bar" for improvement.

CONDUCTING THE INTERNAL ASSESSMENT

Each team conducts extensive interviews with employees and reviews numerous documents within their assigned functional area. These interviews, personal experiences and knowledge of each team member become the driving force for the self assessment.

The Chief Quality Officer coordinates the internal assessment effort and helps to facilitate its progress with calendars and time lines. This effort is simultaneously conducted with all seven teams over four to six weeks.

Teams compile their interview data and documentation data into a comprehensive feedback report that includes:

- strengths
- areas for improvement
- overall scoring
- strategic planning issues

The teams then present the results to the Senior Executive Group for incorporation into the strategic planning process. All levels of the organization have now contributed to the organization's strategic planning process. The Baldrige provides the linkage between the quality process and the strategic planning process.

THIRD PARTY ASSESSMENT

In order to allow for further verification of results, some organizations use a third party assessment to complement their internal assessment process. This verifies the internal data and provides a fresh perspective.

WHAT'S NEXT?

What happens once you have completed the internal self assessment, written up your report and presented the results to Senior Leadership? For some, work begins on using the assessment as an internal tool for improvement. For others, the next step is to submit the self assessment as an application for the Malcolm Baldrige National Quality Award.

We recommend a company that is mature in continuous quality improvement (two to three years for a small business, three to five years for a large organization) should submit the application for the award. Here's why:

Consider the application process as a worthwhile *investment* – with a significant *return* on your investment. When you submit your application, it is initially reviewed by six to eight examiners. However, don't think of them as examiners. Consider them to be *your personal consultants*.

So, you get six to eight World Class consultants who each review and critique your assessment independently. If your company exits out of the examiners review process at any stage, you are guaranteed an extensive feedback report. If your organization is practicing World Class processes, you will advance to the second stage known as *Consensus Review*. Examiners perform a consensus review conference call – a four to eight hour conference call – of your application and how they evaluated it. They discuss their individual perceptions of how they scored each area. This not only guarantees a more representative evaluation, but it also gives you the benefit of a meeting of the minds to discuss what *you're* doing right, and what you can improve upon.

As far as the award process goes, the field of applicants is narrowed to those who receive a *site visit*. If you receive a site visit, six examiners travel to your company's location and perform a complete evaluation, a one week process. A few weeks later, you will receive a lengthy, comprehensive feedback report. To hire an independent consulting group to perform the same study could total a quarter of a million dollars, and that doesn't count the return on your investment.

For example, in only the *initial* stage, each examiner spends at least 25 hours. That's a minimum of 150 to 200 hours.

The Baldrige can help break needs and goals into step by step actions, which lead gradually into making changes in corporate culture. A company should try to integrate the feedback report into its strategic plan and time-line.

Some companies have been able to remedy their problems in one year. It's taken others several years. Regardless of the time, what a gift! The Baldrige assessment is concise enough and on target enough to help many companies remedy their problems in a short period of time. Forget winning – it helps the bottom line!

These measurements can be used as guidelines so a company can make the change. The Malcolm Baldrige Self Assessment provides a powerful blueprint that you can use to transform your organization from quality perceptions to quality improvement and bottom line *results*.

FEEDBACK FROM THE BALDRIGE: STRENGTHS AND GAPS

The Baldrige assessment is designed to provide feedback. Regardless of whether you choose to obtain feedback through a formal Baldrige application process, third party reviewers, or internal reviewers, you will obtain invaluable data for improvement.

A Baldrige assessment creates a framework to help identify strengths to build upon and weaknesses to improve. One organization that conducted a Baldrige assessment identified the following *strengths*. Remember, this fits *their* company, but it may help *your* assessment process to review their findings:

- We have a Mission, Vision and Goals, and our business plans are developed around the goals.
- We have developed, promoted, communicated and rewarded our Operating Values.
- Our Leadership Assessment survey program is being implemented. This effort is key to improving our work environment and allowing all employees to fully participate.
- Our recent Metrics and Re-Engineering efforts are customer-based, rather than internally focused.
- We have a Quality Curriculum, and training is being provided to all employees.
- We have many employee recognition and reward mechanisms in place to support and reinforce consistent quality behaviors.
- We are initiating different relationships with our vendors and suppliers. Applying TQM principles, they are becoming more partnership-based.
- We prototype and pilot all new procedures/services.
- The key quality concept of "ownership" of our customer's problems is deployed and spreading throughout the organization.

This same organization identified areas for *improvement* in the format of actions to be initiated:

- Work processes not documented.
- Cycle-time reduction regarding introduction of new product/services needs to be addressed.
- No benchmarks conducted of "best in class" processes.
- *All levels* of employees, suppliers and customers not involved in our strategic planning process.
- Data analysis needs to be more *user friendly* for all employee levels.
- Customer focus groups that include "end users" need to be organized.
- Identify and develop customer-contact employees.
- Implement a plan for customer-contact employee selection, training and continuous development.
- Partner with critical suppliers; develop a formal vendor certification program.
- Institute *one* "Help Desk" with a single 1-800 number for our customers.
- Institute a formalized improvement action idea system for employees that will ensure timely management response.

If you learn nothing else from this book, remember this – Use the Malcolm Baldrige Application as a Self Assessment. If you win the award, great. But that's not the primary purpose. The bottom line purpose is to make your organization better.

As Cadillac's Grettenberger notes, "If you complete the rigorous application process, and advance to the final stage where you receive a site visit by a Baldrige examining team, you are a winner by virtue of your own, triumphant self examination. While the trophy and the recognition that accompany being named a Baldrige winner are thrilling, I can tell you with all certainty that this intensive self examination required to participate, and the feedback from the examiners, make all participants better companies – better from a product standpoint, better from a customer satisfaction standpoint, and better from an employee involvement and planning standpoint. **The bottom line is, the customer wins.**"

Prior to MBNQA, companies knew there was a void, and they tried many solutions. Often these solutions end in frustration. As an IBM Senior VP notes, "Part of the problem is that we've never had a consistent approach to quality." Their diary reads like this: "In 1979, focus was on product quality, mostly reliability. In 1981, executives were sent to the Crosby School of Quality. In 1984, it was quality in the business process. In 1986, it was work simplification. In 1988, work elimination."

In 1989, they discovered Malcolm Baldrige.

"Management kept changing its definition. The employees were confused and didn't believe management took quality seriously."

The Malcolm Baldrige helped them translate quality goals into specific customer requirements.

Chapter TEN

THE BEST OF THE BEST

Leadership is a difficult word to define. It is a lot like trying to define "quality." It is a word that suggests a realm of possibilities. It is hard to quantify. Are leaders born or made? What attributes must a leader possess? Although there is a difference of opinion among researchers on the set of attributes a leader must possess, one thing is certain – for an organization to be World Class, it must be led by World Class Leaders.

Managers maintain the status quo. Leaders are visionaries and innovators who motivate and inspire their people, and as a result, quality and productivity rise, innovation is more prevalent and risk taking less threatening.

Senior Executive Leadership is an essential element in the Baldrige competition. By focusing on the *behavior* of leaders, the criteria provides useful criteria for organizations to use to measure leadership.

Obviously, no two leaders are alike, but they *do* share certain attributes which are adapted to each leader's set of circumstances. Personality traits among leaders are very different. Some leaders grandstand, some lead by example. Some are very articulate and extemporaneous, others will occasionally read from a prepared text. Some are very outgoing, warm, and enjoy eating in the lunchroom and walking through the plant as often as possible. Others are well insulated from the employees. Leadership is not "one style fits all."

Perhaps one of the difficulties in defining World Class Leadership is that there has not been an adequate tool to measure it. *The Baldrige leadership criteria fills that gap.*

Based on extensive interviews with the Senior Executives of many mid-sized and large organizations, we formulated a list of *Key Characteristics of World Class Leadership*. The characteristics are primarily based on the many qualities and characteristics that were exhibited through our extensive personal interviews with Baldrige winning Senior Executives in IBM-Rochester, Cadillac, Federal Express and the Wallace Company. We believe that these companies represent the core values of manufacturing, service and small business leadership.

- ## Is Charismatic

  We define this characteristic as people-centered, able to persuade or motivate, approachable, hands-on. The charismatic leader provides a vision of quality to which his or her organization can aspire. Charisma is an emotional element and includes the power to influence an employee on initial contact.

- ## Instills Trust

  A World Class Leader elicits trust from both employees and customers. A leader must demonstrate an unwavering commitment to both. It's a written guarantee for customers. It's easy customer access to all levels within the organization. It's the knowledge that all products/services are designed with customer input. It's the employees' sense of opportunity and fairness.

- ## Is Active, Not Passive

  World Class Leaders get things done. They go beyond board meetings. They are members of employee teams. Their actions speak louder than their words. They "walk-the-talk" and model the organization's quality values.

- ## Makes Internal and External Customers the Focus of Each Process

  We saw this over and over again. World Class Leaders view employees as customers. Leaders support their internal customers – the employees. The leaders know that if they genuinely take care of their employees, the employees will take care of the customers. There appears to be a strong *correlation between the level of employee care and the level of customer service*.

- ## Creates Vision

  World Class Leaders think "outside of the box." They create the vision for the company. They see things not as they are but as they could be. These leaders envision future trends and how the company can profit from future trends. Anticipating a new reality is the beginning of creating it. Leaders *anticipate new realities*.

- ## Promotes a Common Language

  World Class Leaders ensure that every employee speaks and understands the same *quality language*. Fred Smith says, "Organizational leaders have to have three things:

  1. a complete understanding of mission
  2. a common set of words, language and phrases
  3. an underlying infrastructure."

- ## Creates a Team-Based Culture

  The leaders we studied use teams to promote employee innovation, trust, participation and empowerment. Regardless of the company, we found that successful teams have one thing in common – a *defined customer focus*. These teams are the lifeblood of the companies, involving Senior Management, employees, customers and suppliers.

- ## Stimulates Knowledge

  A World Class Leader challenges the employee's intellect, innovation and creativity. Through empowerment, employees have greater decision making opportunities and are provided the tools to solve their own problems. What a difference from the conventional management style with all of the decisions being made in the ivory tower! *Successful leaders coach* their employees to grow, learn from mistakes and increase their knowledge and abilities.

- ## Benchmarks for World Class Success

  Each World Class Leader consistently visits a "best in class." We were impressed by the openness of companies to share information with each other. A successful leader realizes the value of comparing the organization's practices inside and outside of the industry.

- ## Integrates Quality Into the Business Plan

  World Class Leaders merge their organizations' traditional plan with a qu ality strategic plan. For example:

  - IBM – market-driven quality
  - Cadillac – simultaneous engineering
  - Federal Express – customer-driven quality
  - Wallace – team-driven quality

All four were involved in supplier certification.

- **Involves Supplier and Customers in the Quality Process**

  World Class Leaders view suppliers and customers as advocates, not adversaries. They *partner in teams with suppliers and customers*.

- **Embraces Quantitative Measurement**

  Without exception, each World Class Leader we observed believes all *quality improvement is based on measurement*.

- **Develops People**

  World Class Leaders believe that people are their greatest resource. They view money and time spent on training not as an expense, but as an investment in the company's future. Each company we visited not only *invested heavily in training*, but also involved the Senior Leadership in the training.

- **Empowers Employees**

  Successful leaders encourage employees to *make decisions for customer satisfaction*.

- **Encourages Ownership of Quality Values by Employees**

  World Class Leaders encourage employees to *identify, create and own the organization's quality improvement goals*. Quality Values are promoted by Senior Leaders and cascaded throughout their organizations.

- **Rewards Employee Innovation and Risk Taking**

  Leaders *recognize innovation and risk taking* in their award systems, bonus plans, newsletters and videos.

TEN CORE VALUES FOR LEADERS

The Baldrige criteria is based on ten core values and concepts.

1. Customer-driven quality

Based on customer needs derived from customer surveys, customer focus groups and customer councils. Attributes that contribute value to the customer and lead to customer satisfaction form the foundation for a company's quality system.

2. Leadership

Corporate leaders develop and maintain a culture for quality excellence. The CEO empowers Senior Leaders to manage for quality and cascade quality training throughout the organization.

Leadership sets quality values and the tempo of the quality initiative within the organization.

Leadership:

- creates a customer focus
- transforms a vertically positioned organization to a horizontal focus
- directs cycle-time reduction within the organization
- measures process improvement
- provides a strategic focus

3. Continuous improvement

Quality is a never ending process of continuous improvement. Continuous improvement is gauged by involving all employees in charting this improvement within all work units.

Internal and external customer surveys help monitor continual improvement throughout the organization. All areas have documented measurements in which to observe trends within various processes.

4. Full participation and development

Quality improvement requires the interaction of management, employees, suppliers, customers and the community. Customer satisfaction depends upon employee satisfaction and the skills and dedication of the entire workforce. This means an investment in the development of employees.

5. Fast response

This is the increment of time required to respond to a customer's request for products or service. This "fast" response is documented and tracked for improvement within many organizations. A company's success in competitive markets is increasingly tied to its ability to provide faster response to customer's needs.

6. Design quality and prevention

Organizations involved in TQM think *preventative* instead of *reactive*. All processes need to be designed to prevent mistakes, problems and rework. The cost of preventing problems at the design stage is much lower than correcting problems that occur "downstream."

7. Long-range outlook

Quality-oriented companies plan with an eye on customer needs. Achieving quality requires a strong future orientation and the ability to anticipate changing customer needs.

8. Management by fact

Leaders in a TQM environment manage by documented measurement indices (metrics) and trend analysis – not by managing by emotion or "feel good" mentality.

9. Partnership development

Building internal and external partnerships represents a teaming approach with customers, suppliers and community organizations.

10. Public responsibility

Quality-oriented companies consistently take the quality philosophy outside the corporate walls to such organizations as:

- trade associations
- service clubs
- local and state government agencies
- churches
- colleges
- schools

SELF ASSESSMENT FOR WORLD CLASS LEADERS WITHIN YOUR ORGANIZATION

Research by A. T. Kearney, Inc. shows that of 50 factors, *quality* is the one CEO's cite most frequently as critical to competitiveness.
The cost of poor quality is substantial. In manufacturing, it's estimated at 25-50% of sales dollars. In the service industry, it's as much as 40% of operating cost.

Given that a company's level of competitiveness is determined by Senior Leadership, it's critical for your company's Senior Officers to assess themselves. We suggest they complete the following Self Assessment using our *World Class Leaders' Success Factors*.

Name _____ (circle one)

Is a charismatic	Yes – Somewhat – No
Instills trust	Yes – Somewhat – No
Is active, not passive	Yes – Somewhat – No
Makes internal/external customers the focus of each process	Yes – Somewhat – No
Creates vision	Yes – Somewhat – No
Aspires to be the best	Yes – Somewhat – No
Provides a sense of common mission and goals	Yes – Somewhat – No
Promotes a common language	Yes – Somewhat – No
Creates a team based culture	Yes – Somewhat – No
Provides intellectual challenges	Yes – Somewhat – No
Benchmarks for World Class success	Yes – Somewhat – No
Integrates quality into business plan	Yes – Somewhat – No
Involves suppliers and customers in the quality process	Yes – Somewhat – No
Embraces a respect for quantitative measurement	Yes – Somewhat – No
Develops people	Yes – Somewhat – No
Empowers people	Yes – Somewhat – No
Instills ownership of quality values by employees	Yes – Somewhat – No
Rewards employee innovation and risk taking	Yes – Somewhat – No
Entrusts employees to take action	Yes – Somewhat – No
Coaches rather than delegates	Yes – Somewhat – No

SELF ASSESSMENT WORLD CLASS LEADERSHIP ACTION PLAN

Note: Include all of the "somewhat" and "no" responses in your Leadership Development Plan. Example would include:

EMPOWERS PEOPLE

Strengths: Gaps for improvement:
1. _____   1. _____
2. _____   2. _____
3. _____   3. _____
4. _____   4. _____

ACTION PLAN

Short Term: (six months to 1 year)
1. _____   _____Date Completed
2. _____   _____Date Completed
3. _____   _____Date Completed
4. _____   _____Date Completed

Long Term: (1 to 2 years)
1. _____   _____Date Completed
2. _____   _____Date Completed
3. _____   _____Date Completed
4. _____   _____Date Completed

Chapter ELEVEN

A Bottom Line Prediction

Can You Predict a Return on Quality?

It's important to remember that quality is not always a quick fix. It usually requires at least two years and will not have total impact for at least seven years in large organizations. Small companies will experience it within a much shorter time frame because of fewer employees and locations.

After two years, the strategic quality plan should be integrated with the business plan. It typically takes two to seven years to see a return on your quality investment with larger organizations, less time in smaller ones.

Financial Stability as a Baldrige Variable

A frequent criticism against the Baldrige application/award process is that some winners later suffered financial problems. In recognition of these circumstances, Baldrige has created financial indices.

However, not all judges agree with financial criteria. One Baldrige examiner told us, "We're interested in a total quality process, not a company's bottom line. Don't get me wrong. A solid bottom line is important, but profit can come from more than quality processes."

Quality by itself is no financial guarantee. Winning the Baldrige Award does not guarantee long-term financial stability. By the very definition of continuous quality improvement, most TQM companies will experience few surprises. Profitable companies will continue to be profitable. TQM companies having financial difficulty will be in a better position to determine a course of action for recovery.

THE QUALITY SELF ASSESSMENT PROCESS: RETURN OF INVESTMENT

Anytime an organization is thinking about a new program, it's helpful to examine how others have fared with the same process. This is the strongest selling point for using the Baldrige criteria as a quality self assessment/quality improvement plan.

- Ever since *Dobbs International* airline catering service adopted a quality improvement program, it's been one of the most profitable companies within the Dial Corporation family.
- When *Bama Pie* decided to integrate quality into its company, it was on hard times with its major customer, McDonald's, because of inconsistent product in McDonald's fried pies. After undergoing a Baldrige self assessment and implementing quality processes, Bama improved its product consistency so much that McDonald's asked them to make their biscuits, doubling Bama's revenue.
- Since its quality beginning, *IBM Rochester* has increased its productivity by 30% while reducing cycle time by 60%.
- Quality advocate *Cadillac* reduced first year warranty costs by 29% in three years.
- *Federal Express*, a long time quality devotee, enjoys a 95% customer satisfaction rating since 1987.
- The Wallace Company's market share increased from 10% in 1987, when it introduced quality, to 18% in 1990, when it won the Baldrige. During that same time period, on-time deliveries increased from 75% to 92%, with a 740% increase in operating profits.
- 1989 MBNQA Winner, Xerox Corporation, reduced defective parts reaching production by 73%.
- 1988 MBNQA Winner, Westinghouse Commercial Nuclear Fuel Division, maintained a 100% on-time delivery of finished assemblies.
- 1988 MBNQA Winner, Motorola, saved 250 million dollars in production costs in a year.

Many companies happily testify that quality generates an incredible return on investment. It can't be done with lip service or by a token quality person or department. It demands Senior Leadership commitment and total company involvement. But it results in improved products and services, more consistency, greater productivity, reduced wastes, a process to measure quality improvement and, of course, more satisfied customers.

PUBLISHER'S NOTE

MORE ABOUT THE AUTHORS:

Dr. Donn Fisher is the Executive Director of the Mid-South Quality and Productivity Center. He is a popular speaker and consultant in quality-related areas, including the ISO 9000. To contact Dr. Fisher, call 1-901-575-3551.

Fisher has created the resource, *A Simplified Baldrige Award Organization Assessment*, (ISBN 1-879111-51-9) to help employees conduct a simplified assessment of their organization based on Baldrige criteria. The cost is 32.95 and may be ordered by calling 1-615-436-4762.

Dr. Julie Horine is a faculty member in the Department of Educational Leadership at the University of Mississippi. She is a national speaker on the application of the Baldrige Award to Education. Dr. Horine's blend of industry and university experience makes her a sought-after speaker on quality management in both the private and public sectors.

A multiple year Malcolm Baldrige National Quality Award Examiner, Horine is also a certified instructor of Total Quality Transformation. For more information, call 1-601-232-5016.

Tricia Carlisle. A dynamic and resourceful innovator for the 90's, Carlisle's business acumen is far-reaching and diverse. Tricia's background is impressive. Serving as president of a multi-million dollar company, she built a business of quick service restaurants, hotels and retail chains. As a consultant, she has developed and directed award winning creative and large management, communication and marketing projects for several industries. 1-901-682-9880

Stephen Douglas Williford is a writer. He writes, co-writes and edits books and special projects. He may be reached at 1-901-365-9084.

GLOSSARY

Benchmarking – "Best in Class" products, services and practices. Benchmarking can include site visits to organizations, and telephone interviews. The action of identifying a process which you would like to improve, searching for a company with a World Class process, observing, analyzing and adapting it for your own needs. Companies benchmark other companies' departments, practices, policies, management styles, incentive programs, corporate cultures.

Brainstorming – Problem-solving techniques used by employee teams to generate ideas. The purpose of brainstorming is to generate as many ideas as possible within a specified time frame.

Cause and Effect Diagram – A problem-solving technique used to determine the root cause of a work process problem. Some organizations refer to it as a fishbone diagram or Ishikawa diagram.

Control – A work process within a defined and allowable tolerance that has been pre-determined by a process analysis.

Control Chart – A graph that is used by employees to determine if their work process is within prescribed limits.

Conformance to Requirements – The process of adhering to customers' requirements and satisfaction.

Continuous Quality Improvement (CQI) – A basic principle of all Quality Programs to continuously improve processes.

Cost of Quality – The amount of human and/or financial resources used to perform a work-related task, error free.

Crosby, Phillip B. – Author of numerous quality books and considered one of America's quality "gurus." Crosby is credited with creating the concept of zero defects for work process. His 14 steps are used by many organizations as the foundation for their quality improvement process. Crosby quality philosophers are the cornerstone for many service organizations in America today.

Cross-function teams – Teams formed from different divisions or departments to solve or create new solutions to a company problem or opportunity.

Culture – A feeling or attitude created by the environment that results in a unified belief or custom. The values, beliefs and behaviors that employees share throughout an organization.

Customers – The end-user of all goods and services produced within an organization. Customers are both internal and external.

Customer/Supplier Model – A paradigm in which a customer and supplier are team members and work in a partnership.

Cycle Time – The amount of time it takes to perform a specified function.

Data – The collection of facts, information or statistics.

Defect – Products or services that do not meet customers' specifications or requirements.

Deming, W. Edwards – Introduced the concept of Statistical Process Control to post-war Japan in the late 1940's. The Deming prize named in Dr. Deming's honor is an award instituted by the Japanese union of scientists and engineers to recognize and stimulate World Class quality improvement in Japan.

Ergonomics – The evaluation of an organization's facilities and equipment to ensure compatibility between workers and the end product(s).

Efficiency – Documented cycle-time to produce goods and services within an organization.

Empowerment – Employees throughout all levels of the organization are allowed and enabled to respond to customer requests.

Feigenbaum, Armand V. – Is given credit for coining the term "Total Quality Control." He advocates an organization – with systems approach to quality improvement.

Fishbone Diagram – See cause and effect diagram.

Flow Chart – A graphic map of work processes used to document the current situation and detect inefficiency.

International Organization for Standardization (ISO) – Promotes documentation and standardization of all work processes within an organization. Promotes international quality control among all nations.

Ishikawa, Kaori – Japan's leading quality expert. Known as the father of quality circles and employee empowerment. The Ishikawa Diagram is also called a fishbone diagram because it resembles the skeleton of a fish. It is used to illustrate cause and effect.

Juran, Joseph M. – Pioneer in the quality movement. Juran defines quality as fitness for use and advocates a "project approach" to quality improvement. He is best known for teaching the Pareto Principles.

Measurement – The process of statistically gauging an organization's results against their customers' requirements.

Non-Conformative to Requirements – NOT meeting customer requirements or specifications.

On the Job Training Teams (OJT) – A company-wide job function analysis, defines and standardizes job functions throughout the company.

Pareto Diagram – A type of bar chart showing where scarce resources should be applied to reap the greatest gain.

Pareto Principle – Based on the theory that 80 percent of an organization's trouble derives from 20 percent of the problems.

People Side of Quality (PSQ) – People skills, such as team building, social styles and performance management, that complement the technical skills of SPC.

Process – A series of activities linked together to provide a product or service for an end-user.

Process Control – A control device to detect and remove causes of variation to a defined process.

Quality – Conformance to customer requirements.

Quality Circles – Groups of employees who meet to solve work-related problems and present their solutions to upper management.

Quality Function Development (QFD) – Integrates customer requirements into an organization's product and service design.

Root Cause Analysis – Determining and evaluating the primary cause of a problem.

Service Industries – Non-manufacturing industries, such as utilities, schools, governmental, transportation, public utilities, finance, real estate, restaurants, hotels, news media, business services, professional services and repair services.

Six Sigma – Statistical variability measure of near perfection used by Motorola, IBM and other TQM organizations that permits only 3.4 deviations (errors) per million, or 99.99997% error free.

SPC Tools – Pareto Diagrams, Histograms, Attributes Control Charts (np, p, c and u charts), Variables Control Charts (X-R, Moving Average/Moving Range and Individuals Moving Range), Process Flow Diagrams and Fishbone Diagrams.

Statistical Process Control (SPC) – Technique for measuring and analyzing process variation.

Strategic Plan – A detailed plan of action that an organization develops by establishing and defining measurable goals to achieve continuous quality improvement within an organization.

Supplier – An individual or group, either internally or externally, that provides input to a work group or customer.

Taguchi, Genichi – Won the Japanese Deming Prize in 1960 for his work in developing the Taguchi Loss Function. TLF is any deviation from the ideal that causes a loss in quality and therefore an economic loss.

Task and Maintenance – Two processes essential for team synergy. Task gets the job done, the product delivered or the work completed. Maintenance lets individuals know they are appreciated. If a team is malfunctioning, task and maintenance need to be reviewed.

Total Quality Management (TQM) – A management philosophy that focuses on the customer and that defines every business activity throughout the organization as a process that is measured, controlled and improved on a continuous basis. Used nationally to indicate a company's total commitment to the Quality Movement.

Zero-Defects – Error free processes to produce defect free products and services.

RESOURCES

AMERICAN PRODUCTIVITY AND QUALITY CENTER (APQC)
123 North Post Oak Lane
Houston, Texas 77024-7797
(713) 681-8578
Fax (713) 681-8578

AMERICAN QUALITY FOUNDATION
253 W. 73rd Street
New York, New York 10023
(213) 724-3170

AMERICAN SOCIETY FOR QUALITY CONTROL (ASQC)
611 East Wisconsin Avenue
P.O. Box 3005
Milwaukee, Wisconsin 53201-3006
(800) 248-1946

ASSOCIATION OF QUALITY AND PARTICIPATION (AQP)
801-B West 8th Street
Cincinnati, Ohio 45203
(513) 381-1959
Fax: (513) 381-0070

FEDERAL QUALITY INSTITUTE
440 G Street NW, Suite 333
P.O. Box 99
Washington, D.C. 20044-0099
(202) 376-3747
Fax: (202) 376-3765

MALCOLM BALDRIGE NATIONAL QUALITY AWARD
National Institute of Standards and Technology
A903 Administration Building
Gaithersburg, Maryland 20899
(301) 976-2762
Fax: (301) 926-1630

MID SOUTH QUALITY AND PRODUCTIVITY CENTER
22 North Front, Suite 200
P.O. Box 224
Memphis, Tennessee 38101
(901) 575-3500
Fax: (901) 575-3510

REFERENCES

American Quality Foundation and Ernst & Young. *International Quality Study: The Definitive Study of the Best International Quality Management Practices*. Cleveland, Ohio: Ernst & Young, 1991.

Bohl, Don L. *Blueprints for Service Quality*. American Management Association, 1991.

Cadillac. *Information Book*. Detroit: Cadillac Motor Company, 1991.

Cooper, G. E. "Does the Baldrige Really Work?" *Harvard Business Review*, Jan.-Feb. 1992, pp. 138-139.

Coopers & Lybrand. *Quality in Government: A Survey of Federal Executives*. Arlington, Va.: 1989.

Crosby, Phil. *Quality Is Free*. Los Angeles: McGraw Hill, 1988.

DeCarlo, Neil J., and W. Kent Sterett. "History of the Malcolm Baldrige National Quality Award." *Quality Progress*, March 1990, pp. 21-27.

Dobyns, L., and Crawford-Mason, C. *Quality or Else*. Boston: Houghton Mifflin, 1991.

Drucker, P. *People and Performance*. New York: HarperCollins, 1977.

Federal Express. *Information Book*. Memphis, TN: Federal Express, 1991.

Federal Express Manager's Guide. Memphis, TN: Federal Express, 1986.

Fisher, Donn. *The Simplified Baldrige Award Organization Assessment*. New York: Lincoln Bradley, 1993.

Galagan, P. A. "How Wallace Changed Its Mind." *Training & Development Journal*, June 1991.

Garvin, D. "How the Baldrige Award Really Works." *Harvard Business Review*, Nov.-Dec. 1991, pp. 80-95.

GOAL/QPC. Third Annual Symposium, 1992.

IBM Rochester. *The Quality Journey Continues*. Rochester, MN: IBM Rochester, 1991.

Kanter, Rosabeth Moss. *The Change Masters: Innovation for Productivity in the American Corporation*. New York: Simon and Schuster, 1983.

Kearns, D. T. *Values and Direction*. Stamford, CN: Xerox Corporation, 1991. Brochure.

Lienert, Paul. *The Detroit Free Press*, October 21, 1990.

Management Practices – U.S. Companies Improve Performance through Quality Efforts (GAO/NSIAD-91-190). Washington, D.C.: United States General Accounting Office, May 1991.

McKenzie, Kevin. "Quality Reaping Rewards at Fed Ex." *The Commercial Appeal*. February 8, 1993, section B, page 5.

Naisbitt, J., and Aburdene, P. *Re-inventing the Corporation*. New York: Warner, 1985.

Peters, Tom, and Waterman, Robert. *In Search of Excellence*. New York: HarperCollins, 1982.

Peters, Tom. *A Passion For Excellence*. New York: Random House, 1985.

Reimann, Curt W. "National Quality Award Brings Opportunities for Industry." *Business America*, May 9, 1988, pp. 5-7.

Reimann, Curt W. "Winning Strategies for Quality Improvement." *Business America*, March 25, 1991, pp. 8-11.

Schmidt, Warren H., and Jerome P. Finnigan. *The Race Without a Finish Line*. San Francisco: Jossey-Bass Publishers, 1992.

Senge, P. *The Fifth Discipline: The Art and Practice of the Learning Organization*. New York: Doubleday, 1991.

"Small Wonders." *Quality Progress*, Nov., 1992, pp. 33-34.

Smith, Frederick W. "Our Human Side of Quality." *Quality Progress*, October 1990, pp. 19-21.

Special Report, *Business Week*, June 1987.

Stodgill, R. M., and Bass, B. M. *Bass & Stodgill's Handbook of Leadership*. New York: The Free Press, 1990.

Toffler, Alvin. *Powershift*. New York: Bantam, 1990.

U.S. Congress. Public Law 100-107, August 20, 1987.

U.S. Department of Commerce. *Malcolm Baldrige National Quality Award, 1992 Award Criteria*, 1991.

U.S. Department of Commerce. National Institute of Standards and Technology. *Alpha Telco*, Malcolm Baldrige National Quality Award Case Study. Gaithersburg, Md.: NIST, 1991.

U.S. Department of Commerce. National Institute of Standards and Technology. *1990 Award Winner: Cadillac Motor Car Company General Motors.* Gaithersburg, Md.: NIST, 1990.

U.S. Department of Commerce. National Institute of Standards and Technology. *1990 Award Winner: Federal Express Corporation.* Gaithersburg, Md.: NIST, 1990.

U.S. Department of Commerce. National Institute of Standards and Technology. *1990 Award Winner: International Business Machines Corporation Rochester.* Gaithersburg, Md.: NIST, 1990.

U.S. Department of Commerce. National Institute of Standards and Technology. *1990 Award Winner: Wallace Company, Inc.* Gaithersburg, Md.: NIST, 1990.

U.S. General Accounting Office. *Management Practices: U.S. Companies Improve Performance Through Quality Efforts.* May 1991.

Wallace Company. *Information Book.* Houston, Tex.: Wallace Company, 1991.

Waterman, Robert. *In Search of Quality: Quality Through People.* Videorecording. Boston: Enterprise Media, Inc., 1991.

Xerox Corporation. *Information Book*, 1990a.

Appendix
ONE

BALDRIGE FUNDAMENTAL CORE VALUES

The Baldrige criteria is built upon a set of core values that address both customer requirements and organization operational performance requirements.

The ten Baldrige core values include:

CUSTOMER-DRIVEN QUALITY

A basic premise of TQM is that quality is driven and ultimately judged by the customer. Customer satisfaction in products and services provides the foundation for an organization's quality system.

LEADERSHIP

Senior Leadership is responsible for creating quality values and high expectations. It is the personal commitment to quality values and the active demonstration of this commitment that enables leaders to reinforce the values throughout the organization.

CONTINUOUS IMPROVEMENT

Continuous Improvement requires regular cycles of planning, execution and evaluation of all operations and processes of the organization.

EMPLOYEE PARTICIPATION AND DEVELOPMENT

An organization's success in achieving its quality and performance goals depends upon the full participation and commitment of the work force. There is a direct link between *employee* satisfaction and *customer* satisfaction.

FAST RESPONSE

Faster and more flexible response to customer requirements is now mandatory for businesses that plan to survive in the global marketplace.

Design Quality and Prevention

Designing quality into products and services prevents problems and emphasizes "upstream" process interventions.

Long-Range Outlook

A strong future orientation and a willingness to make long-term commitments to customers, employees, suppliers, stockholders and the community allows an organization to achieve quality and market leadership.

Management by Fact

Pursuit of quality and operational performance goals of an organization requires that process management be based upon reliable information, data and analysis.

Partnership Development

Internal and external partnerships help organizations to better accomplish their overall goals.

Corporate Responsibility

An organization's quality system goals incorporates responsibility and citizenship.

The core values provide the linkage between an organization's processes and desired results. If an organization is imbued with the core values, it will obtain results in key performance areas such as:

- Customer Satisfaction
- Customer Retention
- Market Share
- Productivity
- Employee Satisfaction
- Waste Reduction
- Health/ Safety
- Environment
- Cycle Time Reduction

Isadore Sharp of the Four Seasons Hotel describes values as the "psychic core" of an organization. Robert Hass of Levi Strauss asserts that, "Values provide a common language for aligning a company's leadership and its people." The current emphasis on shared values in organizations nationally represents a fundamental shift in how organizations view themselves.

CORE VALUE FRAMEWORK

The core values are embodied in seven Baldrige Award Criteria categories. Conceptually, it is helpful to think of the seven categories within a framework consisting of four basic elements: Driver, System, Measures and Goals. These elements address the following questions:

DRIVER: Where are you going?

SYSTEM: What processes will enable you to get there?

MEASURES: How will you know if you are successful?

GOALS: What are your goals?

DRIVER

Senior Leadership is responsible for creating the values, goals and systems, and guiding the sustained pursuit of customer value and company performance improvement. Category 1.0 is included here.

1.0 Senior Executive Leadership

How do Senior Leaders create quality values and integrate them into daily management? How are the quality values communicated internally and externally?

SYSTEM

An organization's system consists of the well-defined processes for meeting its customer, quality and performance requirements. Categories 2.0, 3.0, 4.0 and 5.0 are included here.

2.0 Information and Analysis

Is the information that is used to guide the company's quality management system reliable, timely and accessible? How is competitive benchmarking used?

3.0 Strategic Quality Planning

How are quality requirements integrated into short-term and long-term business plans?

4.0 Human Resource Development and Management

How does the company develop the full potential of its work force? How are employees recognized and rewarded?

5.0 Management of Process Quality

How does the company assure the quality of its goods and services?

MEASURES OF PROGRESS

The measures of progress provide quantifiable results in areas such as product and service quality, productivity improvement, waste reduction and supplier quality. Category 6.0 is included here.

6.0 Quality and Operational Results

How are quality levels measured and continuously improved?

GOALS

The basic aim of the quality process is the delivery of ever-improving value to customers. Customer satisfaction relative to competitors, customer retention and market share gain is assessed. Category 7.0 is included here.

7.0 Customer Focus and Satisfaction

How are customer requirements identified and how is customer satisfaction determined?

FACTS NOT FLASH

Applicants are evaluated on three dimensions: *Approach,* *Deployment* and *Results.* *Approach* refers to the methods, tools and techniques that the organization uses to achieve its quality goals. *Deployment* refers to the extent to which the approaches are applied throughout the organization. *Results* refers to the demonstrated quality and performance outcomes achieved. All three dimensions must be demonstrated in order to become a Baldrige winner. Baldrige examiners look for the:

APPROACH:

What processes or methods are being used to achieve quality products or services? Are methods prevention-based versus appraisal-based?

DEPLOYMENT:

How broadly has the approach been implemented? In just a few areas?

Results:

What results have been demonstrated? What trends are evident?

There is a critical distinction between data and results for Baldrige applicants. Applicants are expected to show progress over a period of time to show that improvements are sustained.

Naturally, heavy emphasis is placed on quality achievement and quality improvement as demonstrated through applicants' data. It is continually emphasized that "facts not flash" are needed to make it through the screening process.

Appendix
TWO

QUALITY SELF-ASSEESSMENT

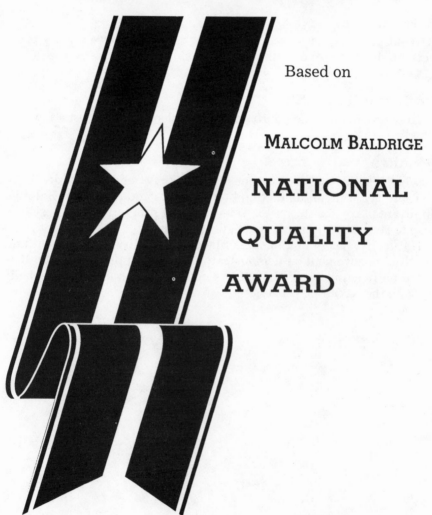

Based on

MALCOLM BALDRIGE

NATIONAL

QUALITY

AWARD

QUALITY SELF-ASSESSMENT

Based on the Malcolm Baldrige National Quality Award Criteria

WHY USE THIS TOOL?

- To introduce yourself to the spirit and intent of each of the Malcolm Baldrige National Quality Award criteria categories through a series of questions. (This tool is not intended to be a replacement for the award criteria.)

- To assess where you believe your organization is currently in the continuous improvement process through the identification of strengths and gaps, scoring, and generation of a radar chart.

HOW TO USE THIS TOOL?

- For each category, read and reflect on the questions. List strengths and areas for improvement on the worksheet.

- Review the scoring guidelines. The guidelines provide a basis for assigning a numerical value to each category.

- Assign a numerical score from 0 percent to 100 percent to each category. Use increments of 10.

- Discuss your perception of the intent of each category with team members. Share your perceptions of strengths and gaps. Reach consensus on the scores for each category. Create a radar chart that reflects the team consensus for scoring.

- Use the radar chart as a departure point for identifying improvement opportunities.

1. LEADERSHIP

- SENIOR LEADERSHIP – How is Senior Leadership personally involved in creating quality values, developing a customer focus, and sustaining an environment for quality excellence?
- MANAGEMENT FOR QUALITY – How are quality values integrated into day-to-day leadership at all levels of the organization?
- PUBLIC RESPONSIBILITY – How does the organization integrated its responsibilities into its quality policies and provide leadership to external groups?

STRENGTHS	GAPS/AREAS FOR IMPROVEMENT

2. INFORMATION AND ANALYSIS

- DATA SYSTEM – What types of data are used to drive quality excellence and how is reliability, timeliness and rapid access assured?
- COMPETITIVE COMPARISONS/BENCHMARKS – How does the organization select and use competitive comparisons and world-class benchmarks to support planning, evaluation and improvement?
- DATA ANALYSIS – How are data analyzed and used to support decision making and planning?

STRENGTHS	GAPS/AREAS FOR IMPROVEMENT

3. STRATEGIC QUALITY PLANNING

- PLANNING PROCESS – How does the strategic planning process (short term and long term) integrate quality and performance requirements? How are plans deployed?
- QUALITY AND PERFORMANCE PLANS – What are the organization's quality and performance goals (short and long term)?

STRENGTHS	GAPS/AREAS FOR IMPROVEMENT

4. HUMAN RESOURCE DEVELOPMENT & MANAGEMENT

- MANAGEMENT OF HUMAN RESOURCES – How do the organization's human resource plans support the quality goals and address all types of employees?
- EMPLOYEE INVOLVEMENT – What mechanisms are available for employees to contribute to the organization's quality/performance objectives?
- EMPLOYEE TRAINING – How are employee training needs determined and what are the trends in quality education and training for all employees?
- EMPLOYEE RECOGNITION – How does the organization's performance, recognition, promotion, compensation, reward and feedback process support and reinforce the quality goals.
- EMPLOYEE SATISFACTION – How does the organization maintain a work environment conducive to the well-being and growth of employees?

STRENGTHS	GAPS/AREAS FOR IMPROVEMENT

5. MANAGEMENT OF PROCESS QUALITY

- DESIGN/INTRODUCTION OF QUALITY SERVICES/PRODUCTS – How are new or improved services/products designed to meet quality and performance requirements?

- PROCESS MANAGEMENT – How are service and product production processes managed to achieve continuous improvement?

- PROCESS MANAGEMENT – How are business and support service processes such as finance and accounting, purchasing, personnel or facilities managed to achieve continuous improvement?

- SUPPLIER QUALITY – How is the quality of materials and services from suppliers assured and continuously improved?

- QUALITY ASSESSMENT – How does the organization assess the quality of its services products? (ie) what is assessed, how often, by whom?

STRENGTHS	GAPS/AREAS FOR IMPROVEMENT

6. QUALITY AND OPERATIONAL RESULTS

- SERVICE/PRODUCT RESULTS – What are the trends for key measures of service/product quality? (ie) internal factors that predict customer satisfaction such as accuracy, reliability, timeliness. How do these compare with competitors?

- OPERATIONAL RESULTS – What are the trends for key measures of operational performance? (ie) indicators such as manpower, materials, cycle time reduction. How do these compare with competitors?

- BUSINESS PROCESS/SUPPORT SERVICE RESULTS – What are the trends for key measures of quality and performance of business processes and support services? (ie) finance or facilities. How do these compare with competitors?

- SUPPLIER QUALITY RESULTS – What are the trends for the important indicators of supplier quality? How do these compare with competitors?

STRENGTHS	GAPS/AREAS FOR IMPROVEMENT

7. CUSTOMER FOCUS AND SATISFACTION

- EXPECTATIONS OF CUSTOMERS – How does the organization determine current and future requirements and expectations of customers?

- CUSTOMER RELATIONSHIP MANAGEMENT – How does the organization maintain and improve relationships with its customers, seek customer feedback, and resolve customer complaints?

- COMMITMENT TO CUSTOMERS – What types of commitments does organization make to customers to promote trust confidence in its services products? (ie) service guarantees

- CUSTOMER SATISFACTION DETERMINATION – How does the organization measure customer satisfaction? How is customer satisfaction relative to competitors determined?

- CUSTOMER SATISFACTION RESULTS – What are the trends in customer satisfaction and dissatisfaction?

- CUSTOMER SATISFACTION COMPARISON – How do the organization's customer satisfaction results compare with those of competitors?

STRENGTHS	GAPS/AREAS FOR IMPROVEMENT

STRENGTHS	GAPS/AREAS FOR IMPROVEMENT

SCORING GUIDELINES

SCORE	APPROACH	DEPLOYMENT	RESULTS
0%	Anecdotal, no system evident	Anecdotal	No data reported or anecdotal
10–30%	Beginning of a systematic approach	Significant gaps still exist in deployment	Some improvement trend data Data are not reported for many areas
40–60%	Sound, systematic approach responsive to the primary purposes Fact-based improvement process in place in key areas	No major gaps in deployment; some areas in early stages of deployment	Good improvement trends reported in key areas Some trends evaluated against relevant benchmarks No significant adverse trends
70–90%	Sound, systematic approach responsive to the overall purposes Fact-based improvement process is a key management tool	Approach is well deployment; deployment may vary among work units	Good to excellent improvement trends reported in most key areas Many trends evaluated against relevant comparisons Current performance is good to excellent
100%	Sound, systematic approach, fully responsive to the all requirements	Approach is fully deployed without weakness or gaps in any areas	Excellent improvement trends in most key areas Most trends evaluated against relevant comparisons Current performance is excellent

BALDRIGE CRITERIA SELF-ASSESSMENT
(Radar chart graphically displays opportunities for improvement)

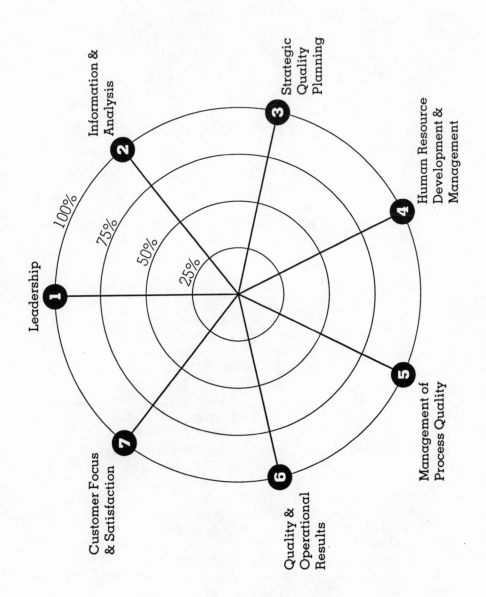

Index

Notes:

Notes:

Notes:

Notes: